Concise First Aid in English

by

ANGUS MACIVER

Edited and arranged by D.A. MacLennan. M.A.

© 1984
ISBN 0 7169 4069 8
Revised 2000

ROBERT GIBSON & SONS · Publisher
17, Fitzroy Place, Glasgow, G3 7SF, Scotland, U.K.

CONTENTS

page

Part 1

Section	1	GENDER	4
Section	2	NUMBER	7
Section	3	VERBS	8
Section	4	PRONOUNS	10
Section	5	ADJECTIVES	13
Section	6	ADVERBS	14
Section	7	PREPOSITIONS	15
Section	8	CONJUNCTIONS	17
Section	9	SUBJECT AND OBJECT	18
Section	10	CONCORD	19
Section	11	APOSTROPHES	21
Section	12	CAPITAL LETTERS	21
Section	13	DIRECT AND INDIRECT SPEECH	23
Section	14	SIMILES AND METAPHORS	24

Part 2

Section	15	ANTONYMS (Opposites)	25
Section	16	SYNONYMS (Words Similar in Meaning)	28
Section	17	HOMONYMS (Words Similar in Sound)	29
Section	18	WORD BUILDING	31
Section	19	CLASSIFICATION	38
Section	20	GRADATION	41
Section	21	GROUP TERMS OR COLLECTIONS	44
Section	22	ANALOGIES	45
Section	23	ABBREVIATIONS	47
Section	24	COLLOQUIALISMS	49
		PROVERBS	53
		DERIVATIONS	56
		FAMILIES	59
		HOMES	60
		OCCUPATIONS	61
		PLACES	62
		SOUNDS	63
		SPELLING LISTS	64
		GENERAL INFORMATION	68

Part 3

TESTS	75

The English Language

In this addition to the First Aid series, the needs of those schools whose approach to English is quite informal have been studied.

The English language was first spoken by various tribes in Denmark and Northern Germany and was introduced into this country when they settled here in the fifth and sixth centuries. The majority of words in English are of this Anglo-Saxon origin but, with the progress of civilisation and continuous contact with other countries, many words are now in common use which have their origin in such languages as Latin, Greek, French, Dutch and German. The words of our language are classified as Parts of Speech and are named according to their functions. This means that every word, dependent on its use, falls into one of the following divisions.

The Noun. A noun is the name of a person, animal, place or thing, e.g., John, tiger, school, kettle.

The Verb. A verb may be said to be a 'doing word', e.g., run, swim, write.

The Pronoun. A pronoun is a word which takes the place of a noun, e.g., he, she, it.

The Adjective. An adjective describes a noun or a pronoun, e.g., good, fine, proud.

The Adverb. An adverb generally gives more information about a verb, an adjective or another adverb, e.g., quietly, here, suddenly.

The Preposition. A preposition shows the relation between one thing and another, e.g., against, for, with.

The Conjunction. A conjunction is a word used for joining words and clauses, e.g., and, but.

The Exclamation or Interjection. An exclamation or interjection expresses sudden emotion, e.g., Oh! Hullo! Stop!

When we wish to express a thought we use words grouped together in a certain order so that we convey a sensible, definite meaning. This combination of words is termed a sentence. In conversation or writing, sentences should always be used in order that the hearer or reader may clearly understand the meaning

---

COPYING PROHIBITED

Note: This publication is NOT licensed for copying under the Copyright Licensing Agency's Scheme, to which Robert Gibson & Sons are not party.

All rights reserved. No part of this publication may be reproduced; stored in a retrieval system; or transmitted in any form or by any means — electronic, mechanical, photocopying, or otherwise — without prior permission of the publisher Robert Gibson & Sons, Ltd., 17 Fitzroy Place, Glasgow, G3 7SF.

Part 1

Section 1 — GENDER

Nouns in English are classed as follows.

Masculine: alive and belonging to the male sex, e.g., man, boy.
Feminine: alive and belonging to the female sex, e.g, woman, girl.
Common: alive and belonging to either sex, e.g., passenger, guest.
Neuter: not alive, e.g., house, pencil.

Masculine	Feminine	Masculine	Feminine
abbot	abbess	bachelor	spinster
actor	actress	beau	belle
author	authoress	boy	girl
baron	baroness	brave	squaw
conductor	conductress	bridegroom	bride
count	countess	brother	sister
deacon	deaconess	don	donna
duke	duchess	earl	countess
emperor	empress	executor	executrix
enchanter	enchantress	father	mother
giant	giantess	gentleman	lady
god	goddess	friar	nun
heir	heiress	governor	matron
host	hostess	he	she
hunter	huntress	hero	heroine
instructor	instructress	him	her
Jew	Jewess	husband	wife
manager	manageress	king	queen
marquis	marchioness	lad	lass
mayor	mayoress	lord	lady
murderer	murderess	male	female
ogre	ogress	man	woman
patron	patroness	monk	nun
peer	peeress	masseur	masseuse
poet	poetess	Mr.	Mrs.
priest	priestess	nephew	niece
prince	princess	papa	mama
prophet	prophetess	proprietor	proprietrix
shepherd	shepherdess	sir	madam
sorcerer	sorceress	son	daughter

Masculine	Feminine	Masculine	Feminine
steward	stewardess	Sultan	Sultana
tailor	tailoress	uncle	aunt
tiger	tigress	widower	widow
traitor	traitress	wizard	witch
waiter	waitress		
boar	sow	billy-goat	nanny-goat
buck	doe	buck-rabbit	doe-rabbit
bull	cow	bull-calf	cow-calf
bullock	heifer	Boy Scout	Girl Guide
cock	hen	cock-sparrow	hen-sparrow
colt	filly	father-in-law	mother-in-law
cob (swan)	pen	grandfather	grandmother
dog	bitch	headmaster	headmistress
drake	duck	he-goat	she-goat
gander	goose	landlord	landlady
hart	hind	male-child	female-child
hold (ferret)	jill	manservant	maidservant
hound	brach	postman	postwoman
mallard	wild-duck	postmaster	postmistress
ram	ewe	son-in-law	daughter-in-law
stag	hind	step-father	step-mother
stallion	mare	step-son	step-daughter
steer	heifer		

Common Gender denotes either sex and the same word may be used both of male and female, e.g., adult, animal, baby, bird, cat, cattle, child, companion, comrade, cousin, darling, dear, deer, fowl, friend, guardian, guest, infant, juvenile, orphan, owner, parent, passenger, pig, pupil, relation, relative, scholar, sheep, singer, swan, teacher, tourist, traveller, visitor.

Neuter Gender denotes things without life or sex, e.g., bag, boots, box, bread, butter, chair, chalk, chimney, church, cocoa, coffee, desk, dishes, door, floor, house, jacket, jotter, kettle, knife, mirror, pencil, ruler, school, seat, stairs, street, table.

Exceptions. We often speak of lifeless things as being male or female, e.g., A sailor refers to his ship as she. An engine-driver refers to his engine as she. A motorist refers to his car as she. An aviator refers to his aeroplane as she.

Names of things that suggest power or dignity are spoken of as if they were masculine, e.g., time, winter, mountains, sun, death.

Names of things that suggest beauty or gentleness are spoken of as if they were feminine, e.g., spring, moon, liberty, peace, nature.

On the other hand, we sometimes refer to a cat, dog, horse, and even a child as 'it'.

EXERCISES

1. State gender of lion, cousin, jotter, mistress, friend, pencil, steward, sister, book, child.

2. Change all Masculines into corresponding Feminines:
    The bridegroom is my nephew.
    The instructor ordered him to jump.
    My landlord is a widower.
    The wizard spoke to the prince.
    The bull attacked the milkman.
    The Duke chatted to the man.
    The heir to the estate is a bachelor.
    "No, sir," he replied.
    The waiter served his own brother.
    "He was indeed a hero," said the headmaster.
    The lion sprang at the colt.
    The master gave instructions to the manservant.

3. Change all Feminines into corresponding Masculines:
    "Well," said her grandmother, "how are you, my little lass?"
    The stewardess brought a glass of water to my aunt, who was seasick.
    The conductress of the bus directed the famous actress to the theatre.
    The proprietrix of the hotel was a wealthy countess.
    The hostess was extremely puzzled by the twin sisters.
    The daughter of a queen is called a princess
    The mayoress talked to the mother of the little girl.
    She was the step-daughter of an elderly duchess.
    Her mother-in-law spoke to the manageress.
    The headmistress rebuked the girl for her conduct.
    She has a sister who is a Girl Guide.
    The girl owned a pet goose.

Section 2 — NUMBER

The Singular Number denotes one and the Plural Number denotes more than one.

Singular	Plural	Singular	Plural
box	boxes	child	children
brush	brushes	foot	feet
fox	foxes	goose	geese
gas	gases	man	men
glass	glasses	mouse	mice
watch	watches	ox	oxen
army	armies	tooth	teeth
city	cities	woman	women
fly	flies	brother	brothers, brethren
lady	ladies	cloth	cloths
calf	calves	die	dies, dice
half	halves	fish	fishes, fish
knife	knives	genius	geniuses
leaf	leaves	shot	shots, shot
life	lives		
loaf	loaves	cannon	cannon(s)
shelf	shelves	cod	cod
thief	thieves	deer	deer
wolf	wolves	dozen	dozen
chief	chiefs	grouse	grouse
dwarf	dwarfs	salmon	salmon
hoof	hoofs, hooves	sheep	sheep
reef	reefs	swine	swine
cargo	cargoes	trout	trout
echo	echoes		
hero	heroes		
potato	potatoes		
banjo	banjoes		
day	days		
halo	haloes		
piano	pianos		
solo	solos		
valley	valleys		

Section 3 — VERBS

A verb is a word which refers to the doing of something, e.g., to run, to smile, to think, to eat. Here are some examples of verbs in action.
1. The sun *shone* brightly in the morning.
2. The lady *is going* home to dinner.
3. The bottle *was hidden* in the cupboard.
4. The patient *should have* rested in bed.
5. The train *will arrive* at six o'clock.
6. Uncle *may be coming* on a short visit.
7. Our neighbours *are having* a party.
8. The ferocious lion *sprang* at the timid deer.
9. The children *were building* a sand castle.
10. The airman *had been captured* by the enemy.

Most of the sentences above contain auxiliary verbs which are usually formed from parts of the verbs 'to be' and 'to have'.

Pick out the verbs, including auxiliary verbs, in the following sentences.
1. The choir sang a Christmas carol.
2. The crew had been rescued by lifeboat.
3. I shall expect a letter from you.
4. The burglar crept silently into the room.
5. The message should have gone yesterday.
6. The tired soldiers fought against heavy odds.
7. The model will be finished soon.
8. The church was crowded at the evening service.

Parts of the Verb

Present Tense	Past Tense	Past Participle	Present Tense	Past Tense	Past Participle
am	was	been	bring	brought	brought
arise	arose	awakened	build	built	built
bear	bore	borne	buy	bought	bought
beat	beat	beaten	catch	caught	caught
begin	began	begun	choose	chose	chosen
bend	bent	bent	come	came	come
bite	bit	bitten	creep	crept	crept
bleed	bled	bled	cut	cut	cut
blow	blew	blown	dig	dug	dug
break	broke	broken	do	did	done

Present Tense	Past Tense	Past Participle	Present Tense	Past Tense	Past Participle
draw	drew	drawn	lay	laid	laid
drink	drank	drunk	leave	left	left
drive	drove	driven	lie	lay	lain
eat	ate	eaten	lose	lost	lost
fall	fell	fallen	make	made	made
feel	felt	felt	meet	met	met
fight	fought	fought	pay	paid	paid
fly	flew	flown	ride	rode	ridden
forget	forgot	forgotten	ring	rang	rung
freeze	froze	frozen	run	ran	run
give	gave	given	say	said	said
go	went	gone	sell	sold	sold
grow	grew	grown	send	sent	sent
hear	heard	heard	shake	shook	shaken
hide	hid	hidden	sing	sang	sung
hurt	hurt	hurt	speak	spoke	spoken
keep	kept	kept	swim	swam	swum
kneel	knelt	knelt	tear	tore	torn
know	knew	known	write	wrote	written

The Present Participle is formed by adding 'ing' to the Present Tense, e.g., beating, beginning, falling, giving, leaving, making, selling, writing.

The Past Participle is formed by adding an auxiliary verb in front of the main verb, e.g., has gone, was sent, had visited, have been lost, were returned.

The Present Infinitive is formed by placing 'to' before the Present Tense, e.g., to bend, to catch, to drink, to fight, to grow, to lie, to ring, to swim.

EXERCISES

In the sentences below select the correct word from each pair in brackets.
1. We (drank, drunk) our tea before we (sung, sang) the carol.
2. After he had (ran, run) about three miles, he (sank, sunk) to the ground.
3. The tree had (fell, fallen) across the road and many of its branches were (broke, broken).
4. He (began, begun) to look for the toy which he had (given, gave) to his brother.

5. The jacket had been well (wore, worn) and the cloth had (shrank, shrunk).
6. After we had (ate, eaten) our supper we went to the pond which was (froze, frozen) over.

Change all singulars into plurals and Verbs into the Past Tense.
1. The rabbit runs from the dog.   **2.** The girl wears a blue dress.
3. The sailor swims to his ship.   **4.** The woman catches the goose.
5. The man shoots the deer.   **6.** The ox eats the potato.
7. The lady prefers the rose.   **8.** The sheep runs into the valley.
9. Her foot is badly cut.   **10.** The thief steals the valuable bag.

Section 4 — PRONOUNS

A Pronoun is a word which takes the place of a noun, e.g., he, she, it.

Personal Pronouns

Nom.	Obj.	* Poss.	Com.	Poss. Pron.
I	me	my, mine	myself	mine
you	you	your	yourself	yours
he	him	his	himself	his
she	her	her	herself	hers
it	it	its	itself	its
we	us	our	ourselves	ours
you	you	your	yourselves	yours
they	them	their	themselves	theirs

* Either Possessive Adjectives, or Personal Pronouns, possessive case.

Relative Pronouns

which	which	whose	—	—
who	whom	whose	—	—
that	that	—	—	—
what	what	—	—	—

Pronouns used as subjects must be in the nominative case, e.g.,
I bought some apples. We saw a large cave.
You will catch a cold. They shouted with joy.

Even the best of us are apt to make mistakes in the use of the double nominative. Study the following examples carefully and note that the pronouns acting as subjects are in the nominative case.
He and I bought some apples. James and you will catch cold.
i.e., He bought some apples and I i.e., James will catch cold and you
bought some apples. will catch cold.

Pronouns used as objects must be in the objective case, e.g.,
The play bored me. The guards pushed you.
The boys will follow him. The lady watched her.
The answer decided them. The children watched her.

Many mistakes are made in the use of the double objective.

Note that the pronouns acting as objects are in the objective case:
The play bored both him and me,
    i.e., The play bored him and the play bored me.
The guards pushed you and him,
    i.e., The guards pushed you and the guards pushed him.
The lady watched Mary and her,
    i.e., The lady watched Mary and the lady watched her.
The children left Sam and us,
    i.e., The children left Sam and the children left us.
The answer decided the captain and them,
    i.e., The answer decided the captain and the answer decided them.

Pronouns used after prepositions must be in the Objective Case, e.g.,
The animal stared at me. The girl will listen to you.
We know nothing about him. A crowd gathered round us.
The policeman ran after them.

Here again the double objective must be watched carefully.
The animal stared at her and me,
    i.e., The animal stared at her and at me.
The girl will listen to you or me,
    i.e., The girl will listen to you or to me.
A crowd gathered round Fred and us,
    i.e., A crowd gathered round Fred and round us.

There are a few verbs which are followed by pronouns in the nominative case where we should normally find the objective. Study them carefully as they often cause difficulty.

First let us understand why these verbs are followed by the nominative. It is because all such verbs make the following nouns and pronouns act in the same way as subjects. For example, all forms of the verb 'to be', when used by themselves (am, is, are, was, were, have been, will be, etc.), control the following pronouns.

It is I. Universal practice allows it is me to be accepted.
    It is she *not* It is her.   It is he *not* It is him.
    It is we *not* It is us.   It is they *not* It is them.

From this we gather that the following are the correct forms
    That was he. Who was she? Those were they. Who are they?

Included with the verb 'to be' are expressions such as 'is believed to be', 'is said to be', 'is supposed to be', 'is thought to be' and the verbs 'to appear', 'to become', 'to seem'.

The boy is believed to be he, *not* him. The lady is said to be she, *not* her. The man who won is supposed to be he, *not* him. At the concert we were thought to be they, *not* them. It appears to be she, *not* her. It seems to be they, *not* them.

COMMON ERRORS

After 'as' and 'than'
He is as tall as me. *Wrong.*   He is as tall as I (am). *Correct.*
His brother is older than him. *Wrong.*   His brother is older than he (is). *Correct.*

The reason is that 'as' and 'than' are conjunctions (not prepositions). After 'let'.
Let you and I go. *Wrong.*   Let you and me go. *Correct.*
The reason is that 'let' is the same as the transitive verb 'allow'.

After 'between'
Between you and I. *Wrong.* Between you and me. *Correct.* The reason that 'between' is a preposition governing both pronouns.

'It's' and 'Its'.

'It's' means it is or it has, e.g., It's a fine day. It's been a very cold winter.
'Its' stands for a thing that possesses something already mentioned. e.g., The ship altered its course immediately.

'Who, Which and That'.
'Who' refers to persons. 'Which' refers to animals, plants and things. 'That' refers to persons, animals, plants or things.

Section 5 — ADJECTIVES

An adjective is a word which describes a noun or a pronoun, e.g., young, pretty, red. Here are some examples of adjectives at work.

> The *tall* gentleman wore a *blue* overcoat.
> *Little* Jim was a *delicate* boy with *pale* cheeks.
> The weather was *wet* and *foggy*.
> The *ugly old* witch spoke in a *hoarse cracked* voice.
> The *lost* ball was found near the *garden* gate.

Comparison of Adjectives

The Positive is used when speaking of or describing an object, e.g., short, big. The comparative is used when comparing two objects and is formed by adding 'er' to the Positive, e.g., shorter, bigger.
The Superlative is used when speaking of more than two objects and is formed by adding 'est' to the Positive, e.g.,

Positive	Comparative	Superlative
big	bigger	biggest
fast	faster	fastest
great	greater	greatest
late	later	latest
long	longer	longest
small	smaller	smallest
tall	taller	tallest
thin	thinner	thinnest
bad	worse	worst
far	farther	farthest
good	better	best
little	less	least
many	more	most
much	more	most
old	older	oldest

Generally with adjectives of two or more syllables, *more* is used comparatively, and *most* is used superlatively. e.g., careful, more careful, most careful.

Positive	**Comparative**	**Superlative**
beautiful	more beautiful	most beautiful
brilliant	more brilliant	most brilliant
cautious	more cautious	most cautious
comfortable	more comfortable	most comfortable
generous	more generous	most generous
gracious	more gracious	most gracious
handsome	more handsome	most handsome
ignorant	more ignorant	most ignorant

EXERCISES

Correct the following sentences.
1. The best team won the football match.
2. Fred was the most fast of all the runners.
3. He proved to be the ignorantest person.
4. Of the two, I like Tom best
5. The sailor lifted the thinnest end of the rope.
6. The patient made the wonderfulest recovery.

Complete each of the following sentences using the comparative or superlative of the adjective given in brackets.
1. The (   ) of the twins is John. (tall)
2. The (   ) girl in the class is Jean. (careful)
3. Weigh both bags and tell me which is the (   ). (light)
4. His right foot is the (   ) one. (strong)
5. He sat in the (   ) seat in the room. (comfortable)
6. I wonder who did (   ) work, John, David or Jack? (little)

Section 6 — **ADVERBS**

An adverb is a word which gives more information about a verb, an adjective, or another adverb. The majority of Adverbs are formed from corresponding Adjectives by adding 'ly':
quickly, bravely, seriously, happily, clearly, quietly, angrily, fatally, suitable.

Here are some examples of adverbs in action.

Dinner will *soon* be on the table.
The man walked *slowly* across the field.
I *once* saw an eagle kill a rabbit.
He can *certainly* boast about his adventures.
There lay the object of our search.
The apples were *quite* good.
Where did you find that knife?
We did *not* go to the school.

EXERCISES

In the spaces provided place the following adverbs:
   stealthily, freely, soundly, angrily, heavily, patiently, broadly, immediately.
1.   The exhausted man slept ....
2.   After receiving his wages the foolish man spent ....
3.   On hearing the good news he smiled ....
4.   Which way should he go? He decided ....
5.   The burglar crept .... into the room.
6.   Making a brilliant save, the goalkeeper fell ....
7.   When he heard of the accident he frowned ....
8.   Although it was raining, he waited ....

Section 7 — PREPOSITIONS

Prepositions show the relationship between nouns and / or pronouns in the same sentence. The following list contains the most common prepositions:
   about, above, across, after, against, along, amid, amidst, among, amongst, around, at, before, behind, below, beneath, beside, between, beyond, by, down, during, except, for, from, in, into, near, of, off, on, over, round, since, through, till, to, towards, under, underneath, until, unto, up, upon, with, within, without.

1.   Use the correct preposition in the blank spaces.
      The boy must apologise .... the lady.
      That man is an authority .... flowers.
      The mother was proud .... her son's success.
      He placed the bat .... the wall.
      My cousin put the book .... the drawer.
      It is an exception .... the rule.

His opinion differs .... mine.
The man ran .... the path.
She takes great pride .... her appearance.
The ball went .... the window.

2. Supply three suitable prepositions in each sentence.
The pencil lay .... the desk.
....
....
The man rowed .... the river.
....
....
The lady sat .... the chairman.
....
....

3. Pick out the prepositions in the following sentences.
I stood on the bridge of the ship
Above me, I saw a cloudy sky.
The dog leaped over the wall after a ball.
We chased him through a field of hay.
With that ticket you can obtain admission to the show.
My brother received a letter from him.
The farmer stored his hay in a large barn.
Beside the boxes lay several boulders.
The careless boy ran behind the car.
During the year many people were injured in street accidents.

Many people find it difficult to choose the correct prepositions. The following should be read carefully and revised from time to time.

According to	comment on
afflict with	complain of
agree to (something)	confer with
agree with (somebody)	conscious of
aim at	defiance of
angry with	despair of
ashamed of	die of
attack on	differ from (opinion)
blame for	differ with (somebody)
change for (something)	disagree with
change with (somebody)	disappointed in (something)

disappointed with (somebody)
disgusted at (something)
disgusted with (somebody)
dislike for
divide among (many)
divide between (two)
equal to
filled with
full of
guilty of
good for
indignant at (something)
indignant with (somebody)
inspired by
interfere with
invasion of
meddle with
opposite to
part from (somebody)
part with (something)
prevail on
protest against
pursuit of
recoil from
regard for
rely on
similar to
suffer from
tired of (something)
tired with (action)
thirst for (or after)
vexed at (something)
vexed with (somebody)
victim of
wait for (person, thing)
wait upon (somebody)
write about (something)
write to (somebody)

Section 8 — **CONJUNCTIONS**

Conjunctions join words, phrases or sentences together. Here are examples of conjunctions in action.

    The boy *and* the girl hurried home.
    She could write well, *but* she could not do her maths.
    I gave him the money, *for* he had earned it.
    Either my brother *or* his chum knows the place.
    Neither James *nor* Mary wants to go.
    The man wiped his feet *before* he went into the house.
    Since I have known her we have been firm friends.
    The boys were going to school *when* we saw them.
    As I was on my way home, I fell.
    Put it *where* he cannot see it.
    We know he was to blame *because* we saw the accident.
    Though the boy had faults I could not but like him.
    Send me word *if* you wish to go.
    He is taller *than* I am.

EXERCISES

In the following exercises there are sentences with groups of two words within brackets. One of the two words is correct, the other wrong. Pick out the correct word.
1. Wait there (how, until) I have finished.
2. We have remained here (whether, since) you left.
3. (After, unless) they arrived, they sat down.
4. The exercise will be corrected (before, when) it is finished.
5. (Until, as) he went up the stairs, he stumbled.
6. There were many trees (since, where) I sat down.
7. The boy is strong and healthy (though, since) he is not tall.
8. She will go (than, if) you ask her.
9. She is older (than, since) I am.
10. The dog ran so fast (that, while) he caught the hare.

Section 9 — SUBJECT and OBJECT

The part of a sentence which tells you what person or thing we are talking about is called the *subject*. The subject is in the Nominative Case. Here are some examples. *John* drove his father's car. Many *people* died in the earthquake. In her hand was a *bouquet*.

To find the subject you must first pick out the verb. e.g., (drove, died, was). Then ask yourself the question 'who' or 'what' before the verb. e.g., (who drove? who died? what was?). The answer to this question is the subject of the sentence.

EXERCISES

Pick out the subject in each of the following sentences.
1. Many rivers flow into the Atlantic Ocean.
2. The little boy ran across the road.
3. Lead is a very heavy metal.
4. He decided to go through the gate.
5. Although tired and weary, the explorers finally reached safety.
6. After the fine weather we had a thunderstorm.
7. On each side of the criminal stood a policeman.
8. In this house once lived a great singer.
9. In front of them lay a yawning chasm.
10. Saddened by our defeat, we returned home.

Section 10 — CONCORD

Concord means agreement or harmony. In formal English we apply this word as meaning perfect agreement between subject and verb. This is shown by the subject and verb having the same person and number.

(a) When the subject is singular, the verb is singular, e.g., He writes. She swims. The baby cries.

(b) When the subject is plural, the verb is plural, e.g., We write. They swim. The babies cry.

(c) Expressions such as *each of, one of, neither of, every one of, not one of* and words such as *each, every, none, anybody, everybody* and *nobody* must be followed by verbs in the singular, e.g., *Each of* the boys *has* a toy. *One of* the ladies *is* married. *Neither of* the brothers *was* present. Is *either* of the sisters coming? *Every one* of us *knows* that it is wrong. *Not one* of the girls *has* a skipping rope. *Each* man *was* searched. *Every* child *has* a secret ambition. *Anybody is* admitted to the caves. *Everybody was* delighted at the close. *Nobody is* displeased with the result. *None* of the ships *was* lost.

(d) A singular subject with attached phrases introduced by 'with' or 'like' or 'as well as' is followed by a singular verb, e.g., The *boy*, with several others, *was* late for school. Alice, *like* Rose, *is* tall for her age. Tom, *as well as* Fred, *rises* early in the morning.

(e) When a verb has two singular subjects connected by 'and', the verb is plural, e.g., The cat *and* the dog *were* great friends. The farmer *and* his wife *are* jolly people.

(f) When a verb has one or more plural subjects connected by 'and', the verb is plural, e.g., The officer *and* his men *were* crossing the field. The boys *and* the girls *are* sure of their work.

(g) Two singular subjects separated by 'either .... or', 'neither .... nor' take a singular verb, e.g., *Either* one *or* the other *has* blundered. *Either* he *or* she *is* right. *Neither* Grace *nor* Helen *knows* anything about it. *Neither* he *nor* she *writes* well

(h) Subjects separated by 'either *plural* or', 'neither *plural* nor', 'both .... and' also 'all .... but' take a plural verb, e.g., *Either* the boys *or* the girls *are* to blame. *Neither* the pirates *nor* the sailors *were* afraid of battle. *Both* Hugh *and* Sam *were* standing. *All but* James *are going* to the picnic. *All of* them *but* Grace *are* correct.

EXERCISES

In each of the sentences below there are groups of two words within brackets. One of the two words is correct, the other wrong. Pick out the correct word.
1. Each of the boys (is, are) going on holiday so each of them (has, have) gone to bed early.
2. Everybody (was, were) pleased as each of them (was, were) treated alike.
3. Neither he nor she (wants, want) to go.
4. (Wasn't, Weren't) we sorry when we heard you (was, were) going.
5. One of the men (is, are) married, and so he (get, gets) preference.
6. Neither of the singers (was, were) present.
7. Both Agnes and Albert (is, are) here to-night.
8. Not one of the boys (has, have) a knife although not one of the boys (is, are) young
9. Anybody (is, are) allowed to enter.

The object of a sentence is in the objective case. To find the object of a sentence, pick out the verb and then put the question. 'whom?' or 'what?' *after* it, e.g., The boy jumped *the gate*. Jean chose *a book*. The leader of the group picked *me*.

Note that not all verbs have objects.

EXERCISES

Pick out the object in each of the following.

1. I bought a camera in the shop.
2. Tomorrow we shall meet him.
3. He broke the record in the race.
4. The boy did the exercise quickly.
5. The hunters attacked a huge bear.
6. Arriving at the house, he met his mother.
7. The police arrested him yesterday.
8. On the bank of the river, the fishermen made a fire.

Section 11 — APOSTROPHES

The Possessive Case of a Noun is shown by a mark ' known as an apostrophe. Here are some examples of apostrophes in use.

Singular Possessive
the lady's bag
the boy's pencil
a day's work
the man's pipe
the woman's glove
the child's clothes

Plural Possessive
the ladies' bags
the boys' pencils
seven days' work
the men's pipes
the women's gloves
the children's clothes.

From the examples given above it can be seen that, in the Singular, the Possessive Case is *always* shown by 's. In the Plural, the possessive case is shown by the *apostrophe* only ' if the plural ends in -s or -es and by the apostrophe and 's, if the plural does not end in 's'.

EXERCISES

1. The boys pencil lay on the floor.
2. The ladies coats were in the cloakroom.
3. My cousins hand was badly hurt.
4. The mens boots were covered with mud.
5. The childs doll fell into the pond.
6. I saw that the object was a womans glove.
7. The register lay on the teachers desk.
8. He looked very smart in page-boys uniform.
9. It took several hours hard work to repair the damage.
10. In the window was a special display of babies clothes.

Section 12 — CAPITAL LETTERS

Here are some examples of the use of capital letters.
1. One day a girl was playing on a busy street. Her ball rolled into the middle of the road and she ran after it. At that moment a motor-car came dashing round the corner. A passer-by saw the girl's danger and ran quickly to her aid. Fortunately he saved her from serious injury.
2. Jean Miller and her brother David are expected to arrive from New York on Tuesday, the second day of October.

3. A man said to his friend, "If you manage to solve the puzzle, send me the answer". His companion replied, "I will send you my solution before the end of the week".
4. The famous collection of Indian animal stories called *The Jungle Book* was written by Rudyard Kipling.
5. I wandered lonely as a cloud
    That floats on high o'er vales and hills
When all at once I saw a crowd,
    A host of golden daffodils,
Beside the lake beneath the trees,
    Fluttering and dancing in the breeze.
6. "Oh!" shouted the boy, "I have hurt my finger".
"Indeed!" exclaimed his father, "You are lucky to get off so lightly".
7. After Jesus had preached to the multitude He proceeded on His way to Jerusalem.
8. He advised me to travel by bus but I told him that I preferred to travel by rail.

From the above examples it can be seen that capital letters are used,
1. To begin sentences.
2. To begin Proper nouns.
3. To begin direct speech.
4. To begin words in titles.
5. To begin lines of poetry.
6. To begin words of exclamation.
7. To begin words He, Him, His, if they refer to God or Christ.
8. To write the word "I".

EXERCISES

Rewrite the following using capital letters where necessary.
1. london is the capital city of great britain.
2. "come here at once," he said.
3. although he was a strong swimmer, he nearly drowned.
4. when i hit him he exclaimed, "ouch!".
5. with a sash of crimson velvet and a diamond-hilted sword, and a silver whistle about my neck secured to a golden cord.
6. the author of "treasure island" was robert louis stevenson.
7. you can sail down the firth of clyde on a sunday.
8. the policeman said to me, "you cannot park here, sir".
9. algy met a bear,
   the bear met algy
   the bear was bulgy
   the bulge was algy.
10. I shall begin my holidays on the first wednesday in july.

Section 13 — **DIRECT and INDIRECT SPEECH**

Direct speech means the words that have actually been spoken by someone, e.g., "Monday is my lucky day," she said.

Indirect speech is what we are told when someone is reporting what has been said, e.g., She said that Monday was her lucky day. Here are some more examples.

> "Are you tired?" Jack asked me .... *Direct*
> Jack asked me if I was tired .... *Indirect*
> "I feel very pleased to be here," he said .... *Direct*
> He said that he felt very pleased to be there .... *Indirect*
> "We must see this film," said Jack .... *Direct*
> Jack said that they would have to see that film ...... *Indirect*

EXERCISES

Change the following sentences into indirect speech.
1. "We must leave as it is very late," said Tom.
2. "We are going to cross the river," said Bill.
3. "1 have been president of the company for three years," he said.
4. The warden said to me, "You are not allowed to park here".
5. "1 think they have made a mistake," said the official.
6. "This is not the way out," I said to my companion.
7. "I'm afraid I don't know," he said.
8. Tom remarked, "I wonder why John is doing that?"

Change the following sentences into direct speech.
1. They were all glad that the weather had cleared up.
2. The clerk said that the train had gone.
3. The little boy asked his mother to give him an apple.
4. John said that he was going to the game.
5. Father said that he would take them to the seaside.
6. The girl asked if she could have a bag of rolls.
7. Mother said that Jean and she would miss the bus if they didn't hurry.
8. The doorman told John and Bill that the film was not suitable.

Section 14 — SIMILES and METAPHORS

A Simile is a figure of speech in which we state that one thing is *like* another or *as* another in one particular respect, e.g., He is *as stubborn as a mule*. His hands were *as cold as ice*. She is *as quiet as a mouse*. The wrestler is *as strong as an ox*. He is *like a lion* in battle.

EXERCISES

Pick out the similes in the following sentences.
1. Throughout the long day he was as busy as a bee.
2. After going on a diet, the woman became as thin as a rake.
3. When I suddenly appeared he stood still, as if rooted to the spot.
4. The huge jet rose like a bird.
5. When on parade the soldier stood as straight as a ramrod.
6. The lake lay as smooth as glass in the morning sun.
7. The twins were as like as two peas.
8. The coward was trembling like a leaf.

METAPHORS

A metaphor is a stronger form of comparison than a simile, e.g.,

He is *as stubborn as a mule*.	*Simile*
He *is a mule*	*Metaphor*
My feet were *like lumps of lead*	*Simile*
I trudged on *with leaden feet*	*Metaphor*

Here are some more examples of metaphors.
- Not winning the prize *broke her heart*.
- If help does not come *we are all in the same boat*.
- When I talk to him all my words *go in one ear and out the other*.
- The screams of the injured *froze my blood*.

EXERCISES

Pick out the metaphors from the following sentences.
1. The leader of the gang was rotten to the core.
2. When the door slowly opened my flesh crept.
3. If you work all the time you get into a rut.
4. I climbed the steep cliff, my heart in my mouth.
5. In the last week of a term the hours creep slowly by.
6. Trying to tie on the fishing flies his fingers were all thumbs.

Part 2 — Reference Section

Section 15 — ANTONYMS

A list of common words with opposites.

abroad — home	chubby — lean	empty — full
absence — presence	clean — dirty	enemy — friend
accept — refuse	clever — stupid	entrance — exit
adult — juvenile	coarse — smooth	evening — morning
ancestor — descendant	cold — hot	ever — never
alive — dead	come — go	everywhere — nowhere
ancient — modern	conceal — reveal	exit — entrance
answer — question	condemn — approve	expand — contract
arrive — depart	confined — freed	failure — success
asleep — awake	confirm — deny	faint — distinct
assemble — disperse	contract — expand	fair — dark
back — front	correct — wrong	fair play — foul play
backward — forward	coward — hero	false — true
bad — good	curse — bless	familiar — strange
barren — fertile	depart — arrive	famous — unknown
beautiful — ugly	depth — height	fancy — plain
bent — straight	die — live	far — near
better — worse	difficult — easy	fat — thin
big — little	dirty — clean	feeble — powerful
bitter — sweet	disperse — assemble	fertile — barren
black — white	divide — multiply	few — many
bless — curse	drunk — sober	first — last
bold — timid	dry — wet	flow — ebb
bottom — top	down — up	foe — friend
bow — stern	dull — bright	foolish — wise
bright — dull	dwarf — giant	foreign — native
broad — narrow	early — late	found — lost
buy — sell	east — west	free — captive
captive — free	easy — difficult	freedom — captivity
captivity — freedom	ebb — flow	go — come
cheap — dear	educated — ignorant	good — bad

25

guilty — innocent	minimum — maximum	purchase — sell
hard — soft	merry — sad	quiet — noisy
hate — love	maximum — minimum	rapid — slow
heavy — light	minority — majority	retreat — advance
height — depth	miser — spendthrift	right — wrong
hell — heaven	miserable — joyful	sadness — joy
here — there	modern — ancient	safety — danger
hero — coward	never — ever	small — large
heroic — cowardly	new — old	smart — slovenly
hide — show	night — day	slow — fast
high — low	noise — silence	solid — liquid
hollow — solid	none — all	sour — fresh
home — away	north — south	spacious — confined
honest — dishonest	nowhere — everywhere	stale — fresh
hot — cold	numerous — scanty	stationary — moving
humble — proud	often — seldom	steep — gentle
ignorant — educated	old — young	summer — winter
immense — tiny	opaque — transparent	take — give
inferior — superior	open — shut	tall — short
innocent — guilty	out — in	tame — wild
join — separate	past — present	truth — lie
junior — senior	peace — war	unite — scatter
juvenile — adult	pedestrian — motorist	vacant — full
land — sea	permanent — temporary	vague — definite
last — first	plain — fancy	valley — hill
late — early	pleasant — rude	wane — wax
lean — fat	plural — singular	weak — strong
liberty — captivity	polite — rude	youth — age
light — heavy	poor — rich	
live — die	poverty — wealth	
long — short	powerful — feeble	
lost — found	praise — blame	
love — hate	present — past	
loud — quiet	private — public	
low — high	prosperity — poverty	
mad — sane	proud — humble	

The opposite by adding a prefix

advantage — disadvantage
approve — disapprove
audible — inaudible
aware — unaware
behave — misbehave
comfortable — uncomfortable
common — uncommon
connect — disconnect
content — discontent
convenient — inconvenient
correct — incorrect
direct — indirect
educated — uneducated
essential — inessential
fair — unfair
famous — infamous
fire — misfire
happy — unhappy
honest — dishonest
human — inhuman
just — unjust
kind — unkind
known — unknown
legal — illegal
like — dislike
lock — unlock
legible — illegible
loyal — disloyal
modest — immodest

moral — immoral
mortal — immortal
necessary — unnecessary
noble — ignoble
normal — abnormal
obey — disobey
order — disorder
patient — impatient
perfect — imperfect
pleasant — unpleasant
pleasure — displeasure
poisonous — non-poisonous
polite — impolite
possible — impossible
proper — improper
pure — impure
regular — irregular
safe — unsafe
sane — insane
reverent — irreverent
screw — unscrew
selfish — unselfish
sense — nonsense
tidy — untidy
transitive — intransitive
trust — distrust
twist — untwist
visible — invisible
wise — unwise

The opposite by changing the prefix

ascend — descend
encourage — discourage
export — import
exterior — interior

external — internal
increase — decrease
inside — outside

The opposite by changing the suffix

careful — careless
cheerful — cheerless
joyful — joyless

merciful — merciless
pitiful — pitiless
useful — useless

Section 16 — SYNONYMS

Words similar in meaning.

abandon — leave
abode — dwelling
abundant — plenty
accused — blamed
acute — sharp
adhere — stick
affectionate — loving
aid — help
ally — friend
amazement — wonder
ancient — old
assemble — gather
astonish — surprise
asunder — apart
beseiged — surrounded
blank — empty
bottom — foot
brandish — wave
bright — shining
broad — wide
caution — care
circular — round
clergyman — minister
coarse — rough
commence — begin
comprehend — understand
conceal — hide
constable — policeman
conversation — talk
courage — bravery
crystal — glass
cunning — sly
curb — control
custom — habit
deceive — cheat
decline — refuse
difficult — hard

diligent — steady
disaster — calamity
dusk — twilight
elude — escape
enemy — foe
encircle — surround
enormous — gigantic
extended — enlarged
exterior — outside
fall — drop
famous — noted
fatigue — weariness
feeble — weak
gap — hole
glance — look
glaring — look
glaring — dazzling
gravely — sternly
greeted — saluted
gruff — harsh
halt — stop
hearth — fireside
heroic — brave
hoax — trick
imitate — copy
insolent — rude
intention — purpose
interior — inside
join — unite
just — honest
lament — grieve
lean — thin
lofty — high
loyal — true
mad — insane
malady — disease
margin — edge

mariner — sailor
marsh — swamp
maximum — most
meagre — scanty
menace — threaten
minimum — least
mischief — harm
moan — groan
modern — new
moisture — dampness
mute — dumb
myth — fable
nimble — active
noisy — rowdy
odd — peculiar
odour — smell
omen — sign
option — choice
painful — sore
peculiar — strange
persuade — coax
plume — feather
profit — gain
prohibit — forbid
prompt — quick
powerful — strong
promised — avowed
protect — guard
puny — weak
purchase — buy
quaint — odd
quantity — amount
raiment — clothes
ramble — roam
rank — position
rapid — quick
regret — sorrow

remedy — cure	squirming — wriggling	transparent — clear
request — desire	steed — horse	unite — join
residence — dwelling	stern — strict	vacant — empty
reveal — show	stubborn — obstinate	valour — bravery
roam — wander	sturdy — strong	vanquish — defeat
robust — strong	surrender — yield	wealth — riches
scene—sight	suspend — hang	wicked — sinful
shrine — tomb	terror — fear	withdraw — retire
sleek — smooth	tested — tried	wrath — anger
slender — slim	thrust — pushed	wretched — miserable
small — little	tranquil — peaceful	yearly — annually.

Section 17 — HOMONYMS

Similar sounding words

air	heir	ceiling	sealing
aisle	isle	cellar	seller
alley	ally	cereal	serial
allowed	aloud	cheap	cheep
altar	alter	check	cheque
ant	aunt	coarse	course
ascent	assent	cord	chord
ate	eight	core	corps
bad	bade	council	counsel
bail	bale	crews	cruise
ball	bawl	currant	current
bare	bear	dear	deer
beach	beech	desert	dessert
beer	bier	die	dye
berth	birth	draft	draught
blew	blue	ewe	you (yew)
boar	bore	faint	feint
board	bored	fair	fare
bough	bow	feat	feet
boy	buoy	flew	flue
buy	by (bye)	flour	flower
cede	seed		

fool	full	muscle	mussel
fore	four	none	nun
foul	fowl	oar	o'er (ore)
gait	gate	pail	pale
gamble	gambol	pain	pane
gilt	guilt	pair	pare (pear)
grate	great	pause	paws
groan	grown	peace	piece
hail	hale	peak	peek
fair	fare	peal	peel
hall	haul	pearl	peril
hear	here	peer	pier
heard	herd	picture	pitcher
hew	hue	place	plaice
higher	hire	plain	plane
him	hymn	plum	plumb
hoard	horde	pores	pours
hole	whole	practice	practise
holy	wholly	praise	prays (preys)
hour	our	principal	principle
key	quay	profit	prophet
knead	need	queue	cue
knew	new	rains	reigns (reins)
knight	night	raise	rays (raze)
knot	not	read	reed
know	no	real	reel
knows	nose	right	rite
lair	layer		wright
leak	leek		write
lightening	lightning	ring	wring
loan	lone	road	rode (rowed)
loot	lute	role	roll
maid	made	root	route
mail	male	rose	rows
main	mane	rough	ruff
maize	maze	rye	wry
mare	mayor	sail	sale
meat	meet	scene	seen
medal	meddle	sea	see
mews	muse	seam	seem
might	mite	sew	so (sow)
missed	mist		
more	mower		

sight	site	team	teem
scent	sent (cent)	their	there
slay	sleigh	threw	through
soar	sore	throne	thrown
sole	soul	tide	tied
son	sun	tiers	tears
soot	suit	time	thyme
stair	stare	to	too (two)
stake	steak	told	tolled
stationary	stationery	vain	vane (vein)
steal	steel	waist	waste
stile	style	wait	weight
sweet	suite	week	weak
tail	tale	won	one
tares	tears	wood	would

Section 18 — WORD BUILDING

Noun	*Adjective*	*Verb*
ability	able	enable
absence	absent	absent
abundance	abundant	abound
accident	accidental	—
accuracy	accurate	—
acquaintance	acquainted	acquaint
action	active	act
actor	active	act
actress	active	act
admiration	admirable	admire
adoption	adoptive	adopt
adventure	adventurous	adventure
advertisement	—	advertise
affection	affectionate	—
allowance	allowable	allow
amusement	amusing	amuse
anger	angry	anger
anxiety	anxious	—
appearance	—	appear

Noun	Adjective	Verb
applause	applauding	applaud
application	applicable	apply
approval	approvable	approve
arrival	—	arrive
ascent	ascending	ascend
assistance	assistant	assist
attendant	attentive	attend
attraction	attractive	attract
beauty	beautiful	beautify
beggar	beggarly	beg
beginner	—	begin
behaviour	—	behave
belief	believable	believe
bitterness	bitter	embitter
blood	bloody	bleed
boy	boyish	—
bravery	brave	brave
breath	breathless	breathe
brightness	bright	brighten
breadth	broad	broaden
camp	camping	encamp
care	careful	care
cashier	—	cash
caution	cautious	—
centre	central	—
change	changeable	change
child	childish	—
choice	chosen	choose
circle	circular	encircle
circulation	circulatory	circulate
civilisation	civilised	civilise
cleanliness	clean	clean ⎫ cleanse ⎭
collection	collective	collect
comfort	comfortable	comfort
commencement	—	commence
comparison	comparative	compare
composition	composing	compose
conclusion	conclusive	conclude

Noun	Adjective	Verb
confidence	confident	confide
confusion	confused	confuse
contentment	contented	content
courage	courageous	encourage
creation	creative	create
credit	creditable	credit
critic	critical	criticise
cruelty	cruel	—
curiosity	curious	—
custom	customary	accustom
danger	dangerous	endanger
darkness	dark	darken
deceit	deceitful	deceive
decency	decent	—
decision	decisive	decide
depth	deep	deepen
defence	defensive	defend
departure	departing	depart
description	descriptive	describe
destruction	destructive	destroy
development	developed	develop
discovery	—	discover
division	divisive	divide
deed	doing	do
duty	dutiful	—
education	educational	educate
encouragement	encouraging	encourage
energy	energetic	energise
enjoyment	enjoyable	enjoy
entrance	—	enter
equality	equal	equalise
exhaustion	exhaustive	exhaust
expectancy	expectant	expect
explanation	explanatory	explain
expression	expressive	express
faith	faithful	—
falsity	false	falsify
fashion	fashionable	—
fame	famous	—

Noun	Adjective	Verb
father	fatherly	—
fault	faulty	—
favouritism	favourite	favour
fire	fiery	—
ferocity	fierce	—
flight	—	fly
food	feeding	feed
fool	foolish	fool
force	forceful	enforce
fortune	fortunate	—
fragrance	fragrant	—
freedom	free	free
friend	friendly	befriend
frost	frosty	freeze
filling	full	fill
girl	girlish	—
glory	glorious	glorify
gold	golden	gild
grace	graceful	—
grass	grassy	graze
greatness	great	—
grief	grievous	grieve
growth	growing	grow
harm	harmful	harm
hatred	hateful	hate
heat	heated	heat
hero	heroic	—
height	high	heighten
holiness	holy	—
hope	hopeful	hope
horror	horrified	horrify
imagination	imaginary	imagine
imitation	imitative	imitate
industry	industrial	—
information	informative	inform
injury	injurious	injure
interference	—	interfere
introduction	introductory	introduce
invention	inventive	invent

Noun	*Adjective*	*Verb*
invitation	inviting	invite
joy	joyful	enjoy
judgement	—	judge
justice	just	justify
knowledge	knowledgeable	know
—	large	enlarge
laughter	laughable	laugh
law	lawful	—
laziness	lazy	laze
learning	learned	learn
length	lengthy	lengthen
live	lively	live
likeness	likeable	like
listener	—	listen
loss	lost	lose
loyalty	loyal	—
magician	magical	—
magnet	magnetic	magnetise
man	manly	—
marriage	marriageable	marry
marvel	marvellous	marvel
mercy	merciful	—
merriment	merry	—
metal	metallic	—
mine	mining	mine
moisture	moist	moisten
morality	moral	moralise
mountain	mountainous	—
mourning	mournful	mourn
movement	movable	move
music	musical	—
mystery	mysterious	—
nation	national	—
nature	natural	—
neglect	neglectful	neglect
noise	noisy	—
notice	noticeable	notice
obedience	obedient	obey
occupation	occupational	occupy

Noun	Adjective	Verb
opposition	opposite	oppose
patience	patient	—
peace	peaceful	pacify
persuasion	persuasive	persuade
pity	pitiful	pity
pleasure	pleasant	please
poison	poisonous	poison
pride	proud	pride (oneself)
proclamation	—	proclaim
profession	professional	profess
prosperity	prosperous	prosper
provider	—	provide
punctuality	punctual	—
punishment	punishable	punish
pursuit	—	pursue
readiness	ready	—
reality	real	realise
reason	reasonable	reason
rebel	rebellious	rebel
reception	receptive	receive
recognition	recognisable	recognise
relief	relieving	relieve
remembrance	—	remember
renewal	renewable	renew
repeat	repeatable	repeat
repentance	repentant	repent
resentment	resentful	resent
resident	residential	reside
revelation	revealing	reveal
revival	reviving	revive
sadness	sad	sadden
satisfaction	satisfactory	satisfy
school	scholastic	—
science	scientific	—
security	secure	secure
sense	sensible	sense
sight	—	see
selection	selective	select
serenity	serene	—

Noun	Adjective	Verb
service	serviceable	serve
shade	shady	shade
shower	showery	shower
sickness	sick	sicken
simplicity	simple	simplify
skill	skilful	—
softness	soft	soften
sorrow	sorrowful	sorrow
speech	—	speak
spirit	spiritual	—
stealing	stolen	steal
stop	stopping	stop
storm	stormy	—
stream	—	stream
strength	strong	strengthen
striker	striking	strike
student	studious	study
success	successful	succeed
superiority	superior	—
sympathy	sympathetic	sympathise
talk	talkative	talk
teller	telling	tell
terror	terrorised	terrorise
thirst	thirsty	thirst
thought	thoughtful	think
tightness	tight	tighten
trouble	troublesome	trouble
truth	truthful	—
type	typical	type
value	valuable	value
vanity	vain	—
variety	various	vary
victory	victorious	—
visitor	—	visit
warmth	warm	warm
water	watery	water
wave	wavy	wave
weakness	weak	weaken
weariness	weary	weary
weight	weighty	weigh

Noun	Adjective	Verb
width	wide	widen
wisdom	wise	—
wit	witty	—
wood	wooden	—
wool	woollen	—
worth	worthy	—
year	yearly	—
youth	young	—

Section 19 — CLASSIFICATION

All things on earth may be divided into two classes.
1. Animate — *living things.* 2. Inanimate — *things having no life.*

The animate or living things consist of creatures and plants. Creatures can eat, grow, and move about from place to place, e.g., animals, birds, fishes, insects, reptiles. Plants are fixed by means of roots and although they can absorb food and grow they cannot move about from place to place, e.g., trees, flowers. The inanimate or things having no life are fixed, cannot eat, cannot grow and cannot move about from place to place, e.g., stone, cloth, knife.

Every object can be placed in a certain general class either because of its resemblance to other things or because of its purpose or use. The following are general classes, animals, birds, insects, fishes, reptiles, flowers, fruits, trees, vegetables, minerals, liquids, apparel, occupations, places, utensils, ships, games, vehicles, cereals, coins, instruments.

Write one name for each of the following groups.
e.g., iron, lead, copper, silver: (metals)
1. lion, bear, goat, mouse.
2. jacket, blouse, trousers, skirt.
3. canary, eagle, pigeon, magpie.
4. lawyer, butcher, engineer, doctor.
5. beetle, ant, bee, locust.
6. bus, car, lorry, van.
7. daffodil, tulip, violet, crocus.
8. cup, saucer, bowl, plate.
9. flounder, haddock, trout, herring.
10. autumn, winter, spring, summer.
11. shoes, wellingtons, boots, slippers.
12. potato, carrot, beetroot, turnip.

13. hawthorn, palm, beech, chestnut.
14. bread, butter, meat, porridge.
15. bramble, orange, banana, lemon.
16. water, milk, brine, paraffin.
17. wheat, maize, oats, barley.
18. aunt, uncle, niece, cousin.
19. twelve, seven, twenty, eight.
20. football, hockey, rugby, cricket.

In the following lists of words, one word seems out of place. Write down the word you consider is wrong. *No. 1 is done for you.*

1. Rose, daffodil, tulip, cauliflower, carnation. — (**cauliflower**)
2. Hen, hare, duck, goose, turkey.
3. Beech, elm, oak, violet, ash.
4. Slate, gold, silver, iron, lead.
5. Potato, turnip, lemon, carrot, beetroot.
6. Granite, cement, limestone, marble, whinstone.
7. Oats, wheat, scone, barley, rye.
8. Salmon, whale, herring, mackerel, cod.
9. Diamond, emerald, pearl, ruby, sapphire.
10. Glasgow, London, Paris, Madrid, Rome.
11. Ireland, Ceylon, Iceland, Malta, Spain.
12. Tea, coffee, biscuit, cocoa, ovaltine.
13. Rain, sleet, snow, heat, hail.
14. Bacon, milk, cheese, butter, bread.
15. Shield, lance, dagger, gun, spear.
16. Bus, tractor, liner, train, van.
17. Cottage, mansion, palace, bungalow, warehouse.
18. Tomatoes, journeys, excursions, voyages, trips.
19. Birch, turnip, maple, chestnut, pine.
20. Man, boy, master, princess, uncle.
21. Daisy, willow, pansy, lily, primrose.
22. John, Joseph, Jane, James, Jacob.
23. Cupboard, kitchen, scullery, bedroom, parlour.
24. Orange, potato, cherry, apple, banana.
25. Oil, milk, calico, wine, water.
26. Boy, wagon, kitten, girl, puppy.
27. Plate, cup, saucer, bowl, fork.
28. Radiator, violin, flute, piano, cornet.
29. France, Germany, London, Italy, Spain.
30. Elephant, tiger, giraffe, crocodile, horse.

31. Salt, sauce, plate, mustard, pepper.
32. Spinster, lady, niece, uncle, sister.
33. Chair, carpet, wardrobe, stool, table.
34. Baker, miner, tobacconist, draper, barber.

From the words on the right, pick one of the same kind as those on the left. *No. 1 is done for you.*

1. Cap, balmoral, hat   face, boot, *turban*, coat, hatchet.
2. jug, tea-pot, cup   bowl, loaf, hammer, key, door.
3. Stork, hen, eagle   egg, butterfly, owl, nest, mouse.
4. Tulip, daisy, violet   foot, cup, brush, hyacinth, scissors.
5. Eye, nose, mouth   hand, leg, knee, arm, ear.
6. Tin, copper, zinc   basin, aluminium, marble, corn, carrot.
7. Sole, whiting, flounder   chimney, street, raspberry, ship, trout.
8. Chair, table, stool   sofa, pot, door, car, tub.
9. Buffalo, monkey, squirrel   wasp, herring, skunk, canary.
10. Apple, banana, plum   peach, violet, onion, hawthorn.
11. Iron, lead, copper   marble, coal, slate, zinc.
12. Ant, earwig, moth   rabbit, fly, poodle, snake.
13. Sheffield, Glasgow, Manchester   England, Scotland, Wales, Leeds.
14. Steamer, yacht, submarine   aeroplane, trawler, motor, train.
15. Falcon, penguin, raven   grasshopper, maple, stoat, heron.
16. Frock, jacket, coat   blouse, curtain, sheet, carpet.
17. Car, train, lorry   van, liner, canoe, helicopter.
18. Salmon, flounder, haddock   vulture, snail, sole, setter.
19. Tennis, hockey, golf   darts, cricket, boxing, whist.
20. Crocus, tulip, hyacinth   chestnut, cauliflower, emerald, marigold.
21. Cocoa, coffee, water   bread, soup, pepper, sugar.
22. Violin, piano, harp   drum, bugle, guitar, trombone.
23. Cabbage, carrot, potato   lilac, beetroot, pine, pheasant.
24. Barber, florist, draper   milliner, labourer, miner, pedlar.
25. Ankle, foot, knee   head, wrist, thigh, nose.
26. Terrier, collie, greyhound   tiger, spaniel, hyena, lion.
27. Wellingtons, shoes, boots   gloves, trousers, slippers, pockets.
28. Oak, elm, beech   pansy, ash, daisy, lettuce.

Write down the word (in brackets) which has a *similar* meaning to the first three words in each line. *No. 1 is done for you.*

1. Cost, fee, charge   (money, price, silver) — *price.*
2. Mount, soar, rise   (depart, arrive, retire, ascend).
3. Hail, greet, salute   (alarm, habit, welcome, ignore).
4. Vigilant, alert, wary   (aloft, believe, attempt, watchful).
5. Notice, perceive, behold   (provide, observe, advise, obtain).
6. Concluded, finished, ended (commenced, allowed, completed, carried).
7. Peace, calm, rest   (quietness, worry, agitated, movement)
8. Support, help, aid   (abandon, remedy, assist, ignore).
9. Walked, tramped, marched. (chuckled, plodded, glanced, knocked).
10. Conquer, defeat, overcome (bully, retire, vanquish, submit).
11. Edge, border, fringe   (margin, centre, interior, cover).
12. Occupied, diligent, busy (lazy, helpless, indolent, industrious).
13. Hinder, retard, delay   (progress, obstruct, reveal, select).
14. Vagabond, wanderer, tramp (milliner, caddie, collector, vagrant).
15. Desert, forsake, leave   (protect, abandon, pursue, arrive).

Section 20 — **GRADATION**

There are five words in each row. Place them in correct order (smallest first). *No. 1 is done for you.*

1. one, ten, million, thousand, hundred.
   (one, ten, hundred, thousand, million.)
2. minute, week, second, hour, day.
3. cow, cat, elephant, sheep, mouse.
4. kettle, cup, pail, tea-pot, barrel.
5. mansion, hut, bungalow, cottage, palace.
6. table, wardrobe, stool, sideboard, chair.
7. shark, sardine, whale, cod, haddock.
8. hen, pigeon, robin, ostrich, turkey.
9. city, country, town, continent, village.
10. bean, carrot, cabbage, onion, turnip.

11. ocean, river, spring, stream, sea.
12. plum, currant, orange, cherry, melon.
13. piano, trombone, pipe-organ, violin, flute.
14. wallet, purse, safe, vault, handbag.
15. fly, midge, ant, wasp, butterfly.
16. sentence, letter, paragraph, word, chapter.

Here are some harder examples. Grade each group of five words according to the word in *italics* (least first).
1. *sound* — giggled, laughed, smiled, guffawed, chuckled.
2. *feeling* — punched, touched, battered, tapped, knocked.
3. *speed* — strode, galloped, trotted, cantered, walked.
4. *sound* — crooned, hummed, lilted, yodelled, sang.
5. *feeling* — fingered, slapped, patted, caressed, walloped.
6. *speed* — marched, sauntered, strode, walked, shuffled.
7. *sound* — shrieked, talked, shouted, whispered, roared.
8. *time* — looked, stared, glimpsed, gazed, glanced.

ASSOCIATION

Write down the two words in the brackets which are *associated with or part of* the first word in **black** type. *No. 1 is done for you.*
1. **Shoe** (sleeve, heel, handle, sole, paper) — *heel, sole.*
2. **Chair** (Saucer, poker, arm, tongs, leg).
3. **Bed** (mattress, carpet, ribbon, blanket, blouse).
4. **Bath** (book, soap, glove, vase, sponge).
5. **Fireplace** (jacket, refrigerator, fender, oven, stocking).
6. **Tree** (wall, trunk, chalk, bough, lamp).
7. **Clock** (hands, wristlet, face, shovel, cushion).
8. **Flower** (purse, stem, seat, lard, petals).
9. **Bird** (sheet, wings, beak, canoe, factory).
10. **Bee** (sting, mirror, bread, honey, banana).
11. **Knife** (acorn, blade, opposite, handle, coat).
12. **Kettle** (spout, plate, butter, basket, lid).
13. **Window** (spoon, glass, pillow, bullet, curtains).
14. **Car** (chart, anvil, engine, tyres, grate).
15. **Sun** (rays, harbour, sermon, heat, crescent).

16.	Bottle	(handle, paper, chimney, neck, cork).
17.	Rifle	(barrel, trigger, candle, mirror, arrow).
18.	Fork	(cellar, prongs, beggar, handle, blade).
19.	Fish	(fodder, arms, gills, mutton, fins).
20.	Torch	(bulb, furnace, battery, meter, grate).
21.	Door	(model, knob, disease, drawer, hinges).
22.	Bicycle	(pedals, hangar, bowl, pump, gangway).
23.	Pillow	(rug, clip, cloak, foam, pinafore).
24.	Ship	(hood, melody, bridge, trolley, bow).
25.	Aeroplane	(funnel, wings, fuselage, tunnel, paddle).
26.	Horse	(bridle, crystal, branch, mane, horns).
27.	Computer	(foot, disc, sand, mouse, hilt).
28.	Piano	(buttons, fatigue, keys, pedals, pencils).
29.	Potato	(forest, peelings, bark, gown, chips).
30.	Hat	(crown, glue, pouch, brim, picket).
31.	Vehicle	(velvet, brakes, wheels, cotton, scissors).
32.	Window	(cords, pane, basin, inventor, easel).
33.	Boot	(knuckle, hatchet, upper, jacket, tongue).
34.	Pipe	(granite, towel, packet, bowl, stem).
35.	Tree	(fork, telegraph, foliage, muslin, cabbage).
36.	Fruit	(marble, core, turnip, rind, salmon)
37.	Car	(parrot, article, radiator, exhaust, pilgrim).
38.	House	(compartment, gable, cock-pit, scuppers, eaves).
39.	Telephone	(paragraph, scabbard, receiver, needle, kiosk).
40.	Barrel	(fatigue, staves, square, hoops, spokes).

Here are more examples with particular reference to parts of our body and their actions.

1.	Ear	(deafness, cantered, listening, noticed, tumbled).
2.	Mouth	(pushed, strode, glancing, tasting, chewing).
3.	Nose	(smiled, sniffed, walked, odour, roared).
4.	Eye	(sang, lashes, laughed, blinked, swinging).
5.	Face	(folded, smile, yodelled, grin, toddled).
6.	Head	(muttered, sauntered, ache, flying, nodding).
7.	Arms	(trotted, mumbled, folded, waving, chanted).
8.	Hands	(writing, strolling, kicking, wink, clasp).
9.	Legs	(crooned, crossed, fingered, smiling, running).
10.	Feet	(dancing, waving, paddling, shouting, grinning).

Section 21 — GROUP TERMS or COLLECTIONS

The following is a list of group terms in common use.

Animate

- an army of soldiers
- a band of musicians
- a bench of bishops
- a bench of magistrates
- a board of directors
- a brood of chickens
- a building of rooks
- a choir of singers
- a class of pupils
- a company of actors
- a covey of grouse
- a crew of sailors
- a drove of cattle
- a flock of birds
- a flock of sheep
- a gaggle of geese
- a gang of labourers
- a gang of thieves
- a herd of buffaloes
- a herd of cattle
- a horde of savages
- a litter of cubs
- a litter of pups
- a nest of rabbits
- a pack of rascals
- a pack of wolves
- a party of friends
- a plague of insects
- a plague of locusts
- a pride of lions
- a school of whales
- a shoal of herring
- a staff of servants
- a staff of teachers
- a stud of horses
- a swarm of insects
- a team of horses
- a team of oxen
- a team of players
- a tribe of natives
- a troop of monkeys
- a troupe of dancers

Inanimate

- a bale of cotton / wool
- a batch of bread
- a bouquet of flowers
- a bunch of grapes
- a bundle of rags
- a chest of drawers
- a clump of trees
- a cluster of diamonds / stars
- a clutch of eggs
- a collection of pictures
- a crate of fruit
- a fleet of motor cars / ships
- a flight of aeroplanes / steps
- a forest of trees
- a hail of shot / bullets
- a hedge of bushes
- a library of books
- a pack of cards
- a rope of pearls
- a set of china, clubs, tools.
- a sheaf of corn
- a stack of hay
- a string of beads
- a suit of clothes
- a suite of furniture / rooms
- a tuft of grass

People

at a dance	assembly
at a concert	audience
in church	congregation
in the street	crowd, throng
in a riot	mob
in a rowdy scene	rabble
at a football match	spectators

Section 22 — ANALOGIES

Here is a list of analogies in common use.
1. Spider is to fly as cat is to mouse.
2. Sheep is to mutton as pig is to pork.
3. Steamer is to pier as train is to platform.
4. Boy is to girl as man is to woman.
5. June is to July as April is to May.
6. High is to low as up is to down.
7. North is to South as East is to West.
8. Uncle is to nephew as aunt is to niece.
9. Soldier is to army as sailor is to navy.
10. Bray is to donkey as neigh is to horse.
11. Finger is to hand as toe is to foot.
12. Feathers are to birds as scales are to fish.
13. Tear is to sorrow as smile is to joy.
14. Wrist is to arm as ankle is to leg.
15. One is to dozen as dozen is to gross.
16. Arrow is to bow as bullet is to rifle.
17. Cat is to kitten as dog is to pup.
18. Foot is to man as hoof is to horse.
19. Father is to son as Mother is to daughter.
20. Artist is to painting as author is to book.
21. Water is to ice as liquid is to solid.
22. Swan is to cygnet as pig is to piglet.
23. Shoal is to herring as school is to whales.
24. Bee is to hive as cow is to byre.
25. Wing is to bird as fin is to fish.

26. Rich is to poor as ancient is to modern.
27. One is to single as two is to double.
28. Flock is to sheep as herd is to cattle.
29. Here is to there as this is to that.
30. Day is to week as month is to year.
31. Eat is to ate as go is to went.
32. Coal is to scuttle as tea is to caddy.
33. Steam is to kettle as smoke is to fire.
34. Pig is to sty as horse is to stable.
35. Hot is to cold as seldom is to often.
36. Water is to fish as air is to animal.
37. Table is to wood as window is to glass.
38. Food is to hungry as drink is to thirsty.
39. Statue is to sculptor as book is to author.
40. Wheel is to spoke as flower is to petal.
41. Nose is to smell as tongue is to taste.
42. Wrist is to cuff as neck is to collar.
43. Walk is to legs as fly is to wings.
44. Island is to sea as lake is to land.
45. Knife is to stab as gun is to shoot.
46. Picture is to wall as carpet is to floor.
47. Graceful is to clumsy as polite is to rude.
48. Descend is to depth as ascend is to height.
49. Water is to pipes as electricity is to wires.
50. Steeple is to church as tower is to castle.
51. Tree is to forest as sheep is to flock.
52. Shell is to egg as rind is to orange.
53. Constable is to thief as gamekeeper is to poacher.
54. Whisper is to shout as walk is to run.
55. Hearing is to ear as sight is to eye.

Section 23 — ABBREVIATIONS

The following are lists of abbreviations in common use.

1. Abbreviations used *before* a person's name.
Capt.	Captain
Col.	Colonel
Dr.	Doctor
Gen.	General
H.M.	Her / His Majesty
H.R.H.	Her / His Royal Highness
Lieut.	Lieutenant
Maj.	Major
P.C.	Police Constable
Prof.	Professor
Rev.	Reverend

2. Abbreviations used *after* a person's name.
B.A.	Bachelor of Arts
B.D.	Bachelor of Divinity
B.Sc.	Bachelor of Science
C.A.	Chartered Accountant
J.P.	Justice of the Peace
M.A.	Master of Arts
M.D.	Doctor of Medicine
M.P.	Member of Parliament.
LL.B	Bachelor of Laws
Q.C.	Queen's Counsel
R.N.	Royal Navy

3. Other Abbreviations.
A.A.A.	Amateur Athletic Association
A.A.	Automobile Association / Alcoholics Anonymous
A.D.	In the Year of our Lord (*Anno Domini*)
A.1.	First Class
A.M.	Before noon (*Ante Meridian*)
B.A.A.	British Airports Authority
B.A.F.T.A.	British Academy of Film and Television Arts
B.B.	Boys Brigade
B.B.C.	British Broadcasting Corporation
B.C.	Before Christ
B.S.I.	British Standards Institute
B.S.T.	British Summer Time

C.	Centigrade, Celsius
C.I.D.	Criminal Investigation Department
Co.	Company
C.O.D.	Cash on Delivery
Cr.	Credit
do.	ditto — the same
E.E.C.	European Economic Community
etc.	*et cetera* — and the other things
F.	Fahrenheit
G.M.T.	Greenwich Mean Time
G.P.O.	General Post Office
H.M.S.	Her / His Majesty's Ship
H.P.	Hire Purchase
i.e.	*id est* — that is
I.O.U.	I owe you
I.T.A.	Independent Television Authority
Lab.	Labour / Laboratory
Ltd.	Limited
mph	miles per hour
Ms.	Manuscript
N.A.S.A.	National Aeronautics and Space Administration
N.A.T.O.	North Atlantic Treaty Organisation
No.	Number
N.S.P.C.C.	National Society for the Prevention of Cruelty to Children
O.H.M.S.	On Her / His Majesty's Service
O.K.	All right
P.O.	Post Office
P.T.O.	Please Turn Over
R.A.C.	Royal Automobile Club
R.A.F.	Royal Air Force
R.C.	Roman Catholic
R.I.P.	*Requiescat in Pace* — May he / she rest in peace
R.S.P.C.A.	Royal Society for the Prevention of Cruelty to Animals
R.S.V.P.	*Repondez s'il vous plait* — please reply
S.A.	Salvation Army
T.A.	Territorial Army
T.U.C.	Trades Union Congress
U.K.	United Kingdom
U.N.	United Nations

U.N.C.F.	United Nations Children's Fund
U.N.E.S.C.O.	United Nations Economic, Social and Cultural Organisation
U.S.A.	United States of America
v	*versus* — against
V.I.P.	Very Important Person
viz.	namely
w.w.w.	World Wide Web
Y.M.C.A.	Young Men's Christian Association
Y.W.C.A.	Young Women's Christian Association

Section 24 — COLLOQUIALISMS

Colloquialisms are expressions used in common conversation.

The apple of one's eye	— somebody specially dear
Armed to the teeth	— completely armed
A wet blanket	— a discouraging person
Dead beat	— exhausted
In the same boat	— In the same circumstances
Carried away	— highly excited
A chip of the old block	— very like father
Under a cloud	— in trouble or disfavour
Down in the mouth	— In low spirits
Down on one's luck	— in ill-luck
All ears	— paying close attention
At a loose end	— nothing to do
Good for nothing	— useless
Hard of hearing	— almost deaf
Hard up	— short of money
Hard hit	— seriously troubled
Ill-used	— badly treated
Lion hearted	— of great courage
At loggerheads	— quarrelling
The man in the street	— an ordinary man
Up to the mark	— good enough
An old salt	— an experienced sailor
A peppery individual	— a cranky, hot-tempered person
A pocket Hercules	— small but strong

At rest	— dead
A rough diamond	— a well-liked person of rough manners
Silver-tongued	— plausible and eloquent
Golden voiced	— pleasing to hear
Purse-proud	— conceited about money
Out of sorts	— not well
On the square	— honest
Stuck up	— conceited
Thick in the head	— stupid
Beside oneself	— angry
Heavy-eyed	— sleepy

GENERAL COLLOQUIAL EXPRESSIONS

weigh anchor	— lift the anchor
keep up appearances	— have outward show
have a bee in one's bonnet	— have a crazy fancy
put one's best foot forward	— do best possible
sweep the board	— take all
make no bones about it	— be plain and outspoken
burn the candle at both ends	— overdo work and play
have one's heart in one's boots	— be very despondent
have one's heart in one's mouth	— be frightened
bury the hatchet	— make peace
draw the long bow	— tell incredible stories
make a clean breast of	— confess
have a feather in one's cap	— have something to be proud of
set one's cap at	— try to captivate
throw in the sponge	— give up
throw in the cards	— give up
cast up	— reproach
show a clean pair of heels	— escape by running
pull up short	— stop suddenly
wait till the clouds roll by	— await a suitable time
turn one's coat	— change one's principles
pay a man in his own coin	— give tit for tat
give the cold shoulder	— show indifference or ignore
throw cold water on	— discourage

cut a dash	— be very showy
lead a dance	— delude
lead up the garden	— deceive by hiding real intention
keep a thing dark	— hide something
keep one's distance	— stay aloof
lead a dog's life	— have a wretched life
draw the line	— fix the limit
keep one's powder dry	— be ready or prepared
throw dust in the eyes	— deceive
make both ends meet	— manage financially
face the music	— meet the worst
sit on the fence	— avoid taking sides
put one's foot in it	— spoil something
fall foul of	— come against
get into hot water	— get into trouble
take French leave	— go without permission
play the game	— act fairly
hit below the belt	— act unfairly
hold one's tongue	— keep silent
blow one's trumpet	— boast
hit the nail on the head	— be right
kick up a dust	— create a row
bite the dust	— fall to the ground
kick over the traces	— throw off control
knock on the head	— put a stop to
turn over a new leaf	— conduct oneself better
pull one's leg	— hoax
tell it to the Marines	— express disbelief
go through the mill	— undergo suffering
put the cart before the horse	— start at the wrong end
make the mouth water	— cause to desire
sling mud	— slander
nip in the bud	— stop at an early stage
send one packing	— dismiss quickly
play fast and loose	— act carelessly
keep the pot boiling	— keep going
rain cats and dogs	— rain very heavily
raise one's dander	— anger
mind your p's and q's	— be careful about your behaviour
raise the ante	— increase the bet

smell a rat	— be suspicious
take a rise out of	— fool
rub the wrong way	— irritate by opposing
get into hot water	— get into trouble
turn the tables	— reverse the result
back chat	— give impudence
ride the high horse	— be snobbish
let the cat out of the bag	— tell what should be kept a secret
send to Coventry	— ignore as a punishment
haul over the coals	— scold or punish
take the bull by the horns	— act despite risks
strike while the iron is hot	— act without delay
take forty winks	— sleep
chew the fat	— argue
act the goat	— behave foolishly
live from hand to mouth	— live in hardship
hang one's head	— feel ashamed
turn up one's nose	— scorn deliberately
play with fire	— tempt serious trouble
swing the lead	— avoid work purposely
blaze the trail	— lead the way
come a cropper	— fall or to fall to the earth
go on all fours	— travel on hands and knees
horse play	— fooling around
a fine kettle of fish	— a very awkward situation
as the crow flies	— in a straight line
a blind alley	— an approach which leads nowhere
a hen on a hot girdle	— unable to keep still
a cat on hot bricks	— on edge
a far cry	— a long way
a flash in the pan	— a single instant success never again achieved
every man Jack	— every one
on the nail	— at the required time
a storm in a teacup	— a fuss about nothing
back to the wall	— up against it
from pillar to post	— everywhere
a bird's eye view	— a view from above
a busman's holiday	— a holiday spent doing the same as one usually does at work

bury the hatchet	— to be reconciled
saving his bacon	— avoid punishment
dead as a dodo	— long vanished
hard up	— short of money
lock, stock and barrel	— totally
no flies on him	— all his wits about him
not worth the candle	— the end result is not worth the risk
a dead cert	— something sure to succeed
a cock and bull story	— lies
with flying colours	— succeeding brilliantly
a fly in the ointment	— something spoiling a good plan
the lion's share	— the largest part
not a patch on	— vastly inferior
bats in the belfry	— head full of silly ideas
by hook or by crook	— by any means available
square peg in a round hole	— unsuited for job
blue-eyed boy	— favourite
dog in the manger	— obstructive without cause
dog with two tails	— absurdly happy or excited

PROVERBS

Proverbs are popular sayings expressed in a clever, brief manner.

1. A bad workman quarrels with his tools.
2. Absence makes the heart grow fonder.
3. A bird in the hand is worth two in the bush.
4. A cat may look at a king.
5. A drowning man will clutch at a straw.
6. A fool and his money are soon parted.
7. A friend in need is a friend indeed.
8. A great cry and little wool.
9. A hungry man is an angry man.
10. All's well that ends well.
11. An apple a day keeps the doctor away.
12. Any time means no time.
13. A miss is as good as a mile.
14. A penny saved is a penny gained.

15. A pet lamb is a cross ram.
16. A rolling stone gathers no moss.
17. A stitch in time saves nine.
18. As well be hanged for a sheep as a lamb.
19. A small leak will sink a great ship.
20. As the twig is bent so the tree's inclined.
21. As you make your bed so must you lie in it.
22. A wild goose never laid a tame egg.
23. Better half a loaf than no bread.
24. Better late than never.
25. Birds of a feather flock together.
26. Charity begins at home.
27. Cut your coat according to your cloth.
28. Discretion is the better part of valour.
29. Don't carry all your eggs in one basket.
30. Don't count your chickens before they are hatched.
31. Ducks lay eggs, geese lay wagers.
32. Early to bed — early to rise, etc.
33. Empty vessels make the most sound.
34. Enough is as good as a feast.
35. Every cloud has a silver lining.
36. Every dog has its day.
37. Every tide has its ebb.
38. Evil weeds grow apace.
39. Example is better than precept.
40. Exchange is no robbery.
41. Experience teacheth fools.
42. Faint heart never won fair lady.
43. Far from court, far from care.
44. Fine feathers make fine birds.
45. Fine words butter no parsnips.
46. Fire is a good servant but a bad master.
47. First come, first served.
48. Forbidden fruit tastes sweetest.
49. Fortune knocks once at every man's door.
50. Good wine needs no bush.
51. Grasp all, lose all.
52. Great minds think alike.
53. Great oaks from little acorns grow.
54. Habit is second nature.

55. Half a loaf is better than none.
56. He laughs best who laughs last.
57. He pays the piper who calls the tune.
58. He goes a-sorrowing who goes a-borrowing.
59. Hunger is the best sauce.
60. Imitation is the sincerest form of flattery.
61. In for a penny, in for a pound.
62. It's a long lane that has no turning.
63. It's an ill wind that blows nobody any good.
64. Laugh and grow fat.
65. Leave well alone.
66. Let not the pot call the kettle black.
67. Let sleeping dogs lie.
68. Listeners hear no good of themselves.
69. Little boys should be seen and not heard.
70. Little pitchers have long ears.
71. Look after the pence, etc.
72. Look before you leap.
73. Love laughs at locksmiths.
74. Make hay while the sun shines.
75. Misery makes strange bedfellows.
76. More haste, less speed.
77. Necessity is the mother of invention.
78. New brooms sweep clean.
79. No cross, no crow.
80. None but the brave deserve the fair.
81. None so deaf as those who will not hear.
82. No news is good news.
83. No smoke without fire.
84. Once bitten, twice shy.
85. One good turn deserves another.
86. One man's meat is another man's poison.
87. One swallow does not make a summer.
88. Out of sight, out of mind.
89. Out of the frying pan into the fire.
90. Penny wise, pound foolish.
91. Pride goeth before a fall.
92. Robbing Peter to pay Paul.
93. Sauce for the goose is sauce for the gander.
94. Set a thief to catch a thief.

95. Shoemakers' wives are worst shod.
96. Silence gives consent.
97. Spare the rod and spoil the child.
98. Speech is silver, silence golden.
99. Still waters run deep.
100. The least said the soonest mended.
101. The early bird catches the worm.
102. Too many cooks spoil the broth.
103. Truth will out.
104. Two heads are better than one.
105. Union is strength.
106. We never miss the water till the well runs dry.
107. Where there's a will there's a way.
108. When the cat's away the mice will play.
109. You can lead a horse to the water but you can't make it drink.

DERIVATIONS

A Root is a word in its first and simplest form. A word may be built up or have its meaning changed by an addition at either end. The addition at the beginning is known as a Prefix, e.g., dis-agree. The addition at the end is known as a suffix, e.g., paint-er

ROOTS

Word	*Meaning*	*Examples*
aqua	water	aquatic, aqueduct
audio	I hear	audible, audience, audit
capio	I take	capable, captive, capture
centium	a hundred	centenarian, century
clamo	I shout	clamour, proclaim, exclaim
creo	create	creation, creature
curro	I run	courier, current, excursion
decem	ten	December, decimal
dico	I say	edict, diction, verdict, dictator
ducc,	I lead	education, produce, reduce
facio	I make	fact, factory, perfect
finis	an end	final, infinite
fortis	strong	fort, fortify

Word	Meaning	Examples
homo	a man	homicide, human
impero	I command	empire, emperor, imperial
liber	free	liberal, liberty
malus	bad	malady, malice, maltreat
navis	a ship	navigate, navy
octo	eight	octagon, octave, October
pello	I drive	expel, propel, repel
pendeo	I hang	depend, pendant, suspend
pes	a foot	pedal, pedestrian, quadruped
planus	level	plain, plan, plane
plus	more	plural, surplus
porto	I carry	export, import, porter, transport
poto	I drink	poison, potion
primus	first	primer, primitive, Prime Minister
pro	before	prospect, prostrate
rego	I rule	regal, regent, regiment
rota	a wheel	rotate, rote, rotund
ruptus	broken	eruption, interruption, rupture
scribo	I write	scripture, describe, manuscript
specio	I see	aspect, prospect, spectacles
teneo	I hold	contain, retain, tentacles
unus	one	unit, unity, union
vanus	empty	vanish, vanity, vain
venio	I come	adventure, prevent, venture
video	I see	provident, visible, vision
vinco	I overcome	convince, victory
voco	I call	revoke, vocal, voice
volvo	I roll	evolve, revolve, volume

PREFIXES

Prefix	Meaning	Examples
a-	on	afloat, ashore, aloft
a-, ab-, abs-	away, from	avert, absolve, abstract
ante-	before	antecedent, anteroom
ad-, ac-, ar-	to	adhere, accept, arrive
bi-, bis-	two, twice	bicycle, biped, bisect, biscuit
circum-	round	circumference, circuit
com-	together	comparison, competition
contra-	against	contrary, contraband, contradiction

Prefix	Meaning	Examples
de-	down	depress, descend, describe
dif-, dis-	apart, not	different, disagree, disappear
ex-	out of	exhale, export, extract
fore-	before	forecast, forenoon, foretell, foresee
im-, in-	in, into	import, include
in-	not	incapable, inhuman
inter-	between	international, interrupt, interval
mis-	wrong	misdeed, misjudge, mistake
ob-	against	object, obstruction
post-	after	postpone, postscript, post-war
pre-	before	predict, prepare, pre-war
pro-	forth	proceed, produce
re-	back	retake, return, retrace
sub-	under	submarine, subway
trans-	across	transfer, transport, transpose
un-	not, without	unfit, unknown, unpaid, unsafe
vice-	instead	vice-captain, viceroy

SUFFIXES

Suffix	Meaning	Examples
-able, -ible	capable of being	moveable, eatable, incredible
-ain, -an	one connected	chaplain, publican
-ance, -ence	state of	repentance, existence
-ant	one who	assistant, servant
-el, -et, -ette	little	satchel, locket, cigarette
-er, -eer, -ier	one who	baker, engineer, furrier
-ess	the female	goddess, princess, waitress
-fy	to make	glorify, purify, simplify
-icle, -sel	little	particle, morsel
-less	without	careless, guiltless, merciless
-ling	little	codling, gosling, darling
-ment	state of being	merriment, enjoyment
-ock	little	hillock, bittock
-oon, -on	large	saloon, balloon, flagon
-ory	a place for	dormitory, factory
-ous	full of	famous, glorious, momentous

Exercises
1. Underline the **root** parts of the following words and give their meanings: century, December, factory, manual, navigate, suspend, pedal, export, describe, tentacles.
2. Underline the **prefixes** in the following words and give their meanings: anteroom, bicycle, circumference, contradict, forenoon, international, postscript, submarine, transport, unknown.
3. Underline the **suffixes** in the following words and give their meanings: heiress, cigarette, explorer, simply, duckling, careless, maiden, attendant, decorator, courageous.

FAMILIES

Parents		Young
father	mother	baby or child
king	queen	prince or princess
man	woman	baby or child
American Indian	squaw	papoose
bear	she-bear	cub
billy-goat	nanny-goat	kid
boar (pig)	sow	porkling, piglet
buck (deer)	hind	fawn
buck (hare)	doe	leveret
buck (rabbit)	doe	rack
bull (cattle)	cow	calf
bull (elephant)	cow	calf
bull (seal)	cow	calf
bull (whale)	cow	calf
cob (swan)	pen	cygnet
cock (fowl)	hen	chicken
cock (pigeon)	hen	squab
dog	bitch	pup
dog (fox)	vixen	cub
drake	duck	duckling
eagle	eagle	eaglet
gander	goose	gosling
hawk	bowess	bowet
hold (ferret)	jill	hob
leopard	leopardess	cub
lion	lioness	cub
owl	owl	owlet

	Parents		*Young*
ram (sheep)	ewe		lamb
stag (red deer)	hind		fawn
stallion	mare		foal
tiercel (peregrine)	falcon		eyas
tiger	tigress		cub
tom-cat	queen or tabby-cat		kitten
wolf	she-wolf		cub

Adult	*Young*	*Adult*	*Young*
bee	grub	moth	caterpillar
bird	nestling	salmon	parr
butterfly	caterpillar	toad	tadpole
eel	elver	trout	fry
frog	tadpole	wasp	grub

Exercises

1. Name the young of fox, eagle, goose, sheep, pig, goat, cow, horse.
2. Name the parent of fawn, pup, cygnet, chicken, leveret, kitten, owlet, duckling.
3. Fill in the blank spaces *the name of parent or young — as required*.

wolf	....	....	kid
....	foal	bear	....
sow	....	....	lamb
....	gosling	eagle	....

4. Give the names for a young salmon, a young eel, a young cod, a young trout, a young bird.

HOMES

Person	*Home*	*Creature*	*Home*
Arab	dowar	ape	tree-nest
convict	prison	badger	sett, earth
Inuit	igloo	bear	den
gipsy	caravan	beaver	lodge
king	palace	bee	hive
lumberman	log-cabin	bird	nest
lunatic	asylum	cow	byre
man	house	dog	kennel
minister	manse	eagle	eyrie
monk	monastery	fowl	coop

Person	Home	Creature	Home
noble	castle	fox	earth, lair
nun	convent	hare	forme
parson	parsonage	horse	stable
pioneer	waggon	lion	lair, den
peasant	cottage	mole	fortress
priest (eastern)	temple	mouse	hole, nest
prisoner	cell	otter	holt
American Indian	{ wigwam / tepee	owl	barn, tree
		pig	sty
soldier	{ camp / barracks	pigeon	dove-cote
		rabbit (tame)	hutch
Swiss (herdsman)	chalet	rabbit (wild)	burrow, warren
tinker	tent	sheep	pen, fold
vicar	vicarage	snail	shell
Zulu	kraal	spider	web
		squirrel	drey
		tiger	lair
		wasp	nest, vespiary

OCCUPATIONS

Describe in a sentence the occupations of the following

athlete	confectioner	grocer	newsagent
artist	conductor	hosier	nurse
aviator	decorator	ironmonger	optician
barber	dentist	jockey	pedlar
blacksmith	detective	joiner	physician
butcher	doctor	journalist	plumber
cabinet-maker	draper	judge	poacher
caddie	drover	lawyer	policeman
caretaker	engineer	locksmith	porter
carpenter	explorer	magistrate	postman
cashier	farmer	mason	reporter
chauffeur	farrier	matron	saddler
chemist	florist	mechanic	sailor
clothier	fruiterer	milliner	sales representative
clown	gamekeeper	miner	sculptor
coastguard	glazier	minister	seamstress
cobbler	greengrocer	navvy	shepherd

slater	stoker	tinker	wright
soldier	surgeon	tobacconist	
stationer	tailor	tourist	
steeplejack	teacher	witness	

With whom do you associate the following?

anvil	handcuffs	prescription	spanner
awl	harness	pulpit	spectacles
barrow	hats	razor	telescope
baton	knife	rifle	thimble
brief-case	lancet	roofs	ticket-punch
cigarettes	mail	safety-lamp	tins
cleaver	oath	saw	trumpet
forceps	pack	scales	ward
furnace	palette	sheep	wig
glasscutter	plane	shovel	
guide-book	plough	solder	

Name the chief persons connected with the following.

army	hospital	Police Station	school
church	navy	Post Office	ship
college	newspaper	prison	Sunday School
committee	orchestra	railway station	team of players
court of law	Parliament	Salvation Army	workshop

PLACES

Worship. Abbey, cathedral, chapel, church, convent, kirk, monastery, mosque, pagoda, priory, synagogue, tabernacle, temple,

Business. What are the places called where the following goods are made? Beer, bread, films, flour, iron goods, leather, money, paper, ships, whisky.
Name particular places where the following are sold. Bread, clothes, dresses, fish, flowers, fruit, general foodstuffs, hats, meat, milk, newspapers, poultry, spectacles, stockings, sweets, tobacco, vegetables, writing materials.

Sport. Give particular names of the places where the following are played. Badminton, bowls, boxing, cricket, croquet, football, golf, hockey, putting, rugby, running, skating, sleighing, tennis, wrestling.

General. Give the particular names of the places connected with the following.

Where	*Where*
wild animals are kept	clothes are cleaned
bees are kept	films are shown
birds are kept	fruit trees grow
bull-fighting is held	gas is stored
chickens are hatched	grain is stored
criminals are kept	grapes are grown
crows build their nests	historical relics are shown
doctors receive their patients	justice is meted out
fish are kept	operations are performed
orphans are kept	motor cars are kept
people are buried	plays are shown
people lunch for payment	buses are kept
pupils are educated	water is stored
soldiers are stationed	young plants and flowers are reared
aeroplanes are kept	young trees are grown

SOUNDS (*made by Objects*)

Note that the words have been formed to resemble the sounds made by the objects.

babble of a stream	crackling of wood	pealing of bells
bang of a door	crack of a whip	ping of a bullet
beat of a drum	creak of a hinge	popping of corks
blare of a trumpet	crinkle of paper	purr of an engine
blast of an explosion	dripping of water	rattling of dishes
booming of a gun	grinding of brakes	report of a rifle
bubbling of water	gurgle of a stream	ring of metal
buzz of a saw	hissing of steam	ringing of bells
buzz of a telephone	hoot of a horn	roar of a torrent
call of a bugle	howling of the wind	rumble of a train
chime of a bell (large)	jangling of chains	rustle of silk
chime of a clock	jingle of coins	rustling of leaves
chug of an engine	lapping of water	scrape of a bow
clang of an anvil	lash of a whip	screeching of brakes
clang of a bell	murmur of a stream	shriek of a whistle
clanking of chains	patter of feet	shuffling of feet
clatter of hoofs	patter of rain	
clink of a coin		

sighing of the wind	tinkle of a bell (small)	twang of a bow
singing of the kettle	tinkle of glass	wail of a siren
skirl of the bagpipes	throb of an engine	whack of a cane
slam of a door	thunder of hoofs	wheezing of bellows
splutter of an engine	toot of a horn	whine of a jet engine
swish of skirts	tramp of feet	whirring of wings
tick of a clock		

SPELLING LISTS

The following are lists of words under topic headings. They may be used either as aids to writing or for more formal work.

Appearance	*Astronauts*	*Books*	*Buildings*
ankle	altitude	account	apartment
average	atmosphere	annual	block
black	blast-off	author	bungalow
bland	capsule	character	cathedral
blonde	cloudy	contain	factory
brown	flight	descriptive	garage
build	horizon	exciting	hotel
cheerful	launching-pad	fiction	hypermarket
clothes	lunar	funny	mansion
complexion	module	horror	museum
eyebrow	orbit	humorous	palace
eyelash	planet	imagination	restaurant
forehead	propulsion	interesting	supermarket
freckles	rockets	library	tenement
gentle	satellite	mystery	terrace
grey	solar	novel	theatre
hair	spacecraft	suspense	warehouse
knee	space-platform	thrilling	
loud	shuttle	topical	
ordinary			
pale			
plump			
quiet			
reddish			
rosy			
shoulder			
slim			
voice			

Cinema	*Circus*	*Flight*	*Food and Drink*
actor	acrobat	airport	appetising
actress	animals	airship	bacon
adventure	antics	balloon	banana
balcony	arena	cabin	biscuit
beautiful	canvas	controller	bread
brilliant	clown	crew	butter
character	daring	elevators	cake
comedy	elephants	engine	cereals
continuous	horses	engineer	cheese
cowboy	juggler	flaps	chocolate
gangster	lions	fuselage	cocoa
handsome	monkeys	glider	coffee
horror	ringmaster	helicopter	delicious
outlaw	seals	jet	groceries
performance	spectator	navigator	lemonade
sheriff	tigers	pilot,	margarine
stalls	trapeze	propeller	marmalade
technicolour	zebras	radar	porridge
thriller		runway	potato
torch		steward	pudding
usherette		stewardess	restaurant
		supersonic	sandwich
		tourist	sauce
		turbo-prop	sausage
			sponge
			steak
			sugar
			tomato

Games	*Gardens*	*Geography*	*Hobbies*
colours	apple	climate	album
competition	blossoms	country	autograph
dribble	cabbage	cultivate	balsa
equalise	carnations	customs	cardboard
exciting	carrot	discovered	chess
foul	cauliflower	earth	collection
goal	daffodils	earthquakes	decorating
international	foliage	export	embroidery
jersey	gooseberry	foreign	jigsaws
league	hyacinth	forest	knitting
official	irises	glacial	marbles

Games
opponents
pavilion
penalty
position
referee
score
stadium
supporter
versus
whistle

Gardens
leek
lettuce
onion
pansies
parsley
pear
petal
plum
potato
raspberry
rhubarb
scent
sprouts
strawberry
tulips
turnip

Geography
import
industry
island
language
manufacture
mountain
native
peasant
plain
population
prairie
river
scenery
source
surface
trade

Hobbies
model
painting
reading
records
skating
stereo

House
address
attic
bedspread
blanket
cabinet
ceiling
cellar
chimney
couch
crystal
curtain
cushion
cutlery
electricity
furniture
hall
hearth
heating
kitchen
lounge
mantlepiece
settee
wardrobe

Hospital
accident
anaesthetic
appendix
broken
casualty
doctor
fracture
matron
medicine
nurse
operation
plaster
sister
sterilise
surgeon
theatre
thermometer
tonsils
ward

Newspapers
advertisement
advertising
article
cartoon
column
daily
editor
editorial
evening
feature
journalist
letters
photographer
popular
reader
reporter
sport
Sunday
weekly

Occupations
accountant
baker
butcher
confectioner
detective
doctor
electrician
fireman
fruiterer
grocer
ironmonger
jeweller
lawyer
secretary
solicitor
stationer
typist

Pets	*Police*	*Power*	*Radio / TV*
Alsation	assault	atomic	audience
budgie	chase	coal	broadcast
canary	constable	combustion	commentator
collie	crime	current	competitor
goldfish	criminal	diesel	current affairs
greyhound	detective	dynamo	digital
guinea pig	duty	electricity	documentary
hamster	fingerprints	energy	feature
Labrador	force	fuels	interactive
Pekinese	hunt	gas	orchestra
pigeon	inspector	generated	play
poodle	Interpol	generator	programme
rabbit	interrogation	grid	quiz
snakes	justice	Hydro-electric	records
spaniel	Panda	kerosene	schools
spiders	robbery	nuclear	screen
terrier	sergeant	petrol	serial
tortoise	thief	petroleum	series
	traffic	refineries	soaps
	vandalism	source	studio
	vandals	turbines	tape
		uranium	video
		voltage	viewer

School	*Science*	*Solar System*	*Transport*
addition	antiseptic	astronomer	aeroplane
answer	apparatus	atmosphere	airport
attention	barometer	comet	bicycle
comprehensive	chloroform	earth	carriage
correct	computer	eclipse	coach
corridor	discovery	galaxy	cruise
decimal	experiment	gravity	customs
division	germs	orbit	destination
education	hydrogen	planets	engine
English	internet	probe	fare
error	laboratory	satellite	hovercraft
examinations	laser	seasons	luggage
infants	medicine	space-platform	passenger

School	*Science*	*Solar System*	*Transport*
interval	oxygen	telescope	pier
Mathematics	scientist	universe	platform
metric	thermometer		terminal
multiplication	universe		traffic
period	X-ray		
projects			
pupils			
question			
register			
subtraction			
teacher			
term			

Zoo

ape	gorilla	llama	seal
attendant	hippopotamus	monkey	tiger
bear	hyena	panther	vet
camel	kangaroo	penguin	walrus
elephant	keeper	porcupine	zebra
gazelle	leopard	reptile	
giraffe	lion	rhinoceros	

GENERAL INFORMATION

The Races of Mankind are divided according to colour. The divisions in numerical order are:

Mongolian	yellow	Asia
Caucasian	white	Europe (principally)
African peoples	black or dark brown	Africa
Semitic and Malayan	brown	North Africa, India and Malaya
American Indian	red	America

The Principal Languages of the World are as follows, arranged according to the number speaking. Chinese, English, Russian, Western Hindi, Spanish, German, French, Japanese, Portuguese and Italian. The Continents are Asia, America, Africa, Europe and Australia. The Oceans are Pacific, Atlantic, Indian, Arctic and Antarctic. The Largest Islands are Greenland, Borneo, Baffin Land, Madagascar (Malagasay Republic) and New Guinea.

The Greatest Lakes are Caspian Sea (Russia), Lake Superior (North America), Aral Sea (C.I.S.), Lake Victoria Nyanza (Central Africa), Lake Michigan (North America) and Lake Huron (North America). The Highest Mountains of the World are in the Himalayan and *Karakoram Mountain Ranges in Northern India. They are Mt. Everest, Mt. *Godwin-Austen, Mt. Kangchenjunga, Mt. Nanga Parbat and Mt. Kamet. The Longest Rivers are Missouri-Mississippi (United States), Amazon (Brazil), Nile (Egypt), Yangtse (China), Yenesei Congo (Central Africa) and Lena (Russia). The Largest Cities of the World are New York (U.S.A.), Tokyo (Japan), Paris (France), London (England), Chicago (U.S.A.), Shanghai (China), Moscow (Russia) and Berlin (Germany).

VARIOUS COUNTRIES. Their Peoples and Language

Country	*People*	*Language*
Arabia	Arabian	Arabic
Australia	Australian	English
Belgium	Belgian	Flemish, French
Bulgaria	Bulgarian	Bulgarian
Canada	Canadian	English, French
Chinese People's Republic	Chinese	Chinese
Czechoslovakia	Czechs, Slovaks	Czech
Denmark	Danes	Danish
Egypt	Egyptians	Arabic
England	English	English
Finland	Finns	Finnish
France	French	French
Germany	German	German
Greece	Greek	Greek
Greenland	Eskimo	Eskimo
Holland	Dutch	Dutch
Hungary	Hungarian	Magyar
India	Indian	Hindi
Republic of Ireland (Eire)	Irish	English, Gaelic
Israel	Israelis	Hebrew
Italy	Italian	Italian
Japan (Nippon)	Japanese	Japanese
Mexico	Mexican	Spanish

Country	People	Language
New Zealand	New Zealanders, Maoris	English, Maori
Norway	Norwegian	Norse
Pakistan	Pakistanis	Urdu
Persia	Persian	Persian
Poland	Poles	Polish
Portugal	Portuguese	Portuguese
Scotland	Scottish	English, Gaelic
Thailand	Thais	Thai
South Africa	South Africans	English, Afrikaans
Spain	Spanish	Spanish
Switzerland	Swiss	French, German, Italian
Turkey	Turks	Turkish
United States	American	English
Russia	Russian	Russian, etc.
Wales	Welsh	English, Cymric

Origin of Certain Place Names

Asia, the largest continent, takes its name from the district behind Smyrna in Turkey. We sometimes refer to the eastern part of the continent as the 'Orient' (Land of the Rising Sun).

America is named after Amerigo Vespucci, who explored parts of the coastline of the New World, shortly after its discovery by Columbus.

Europe — some say it was named Eref by the Phoenicians, meaning "The Land of the Setting Sun" and sometimes referred to as the "Occident". Others say it was named after Europus, a town in Macedonia.

Africa was named by the Romans after the Afri tribe of Tunisia.

Australia means the "Southern Continent".

Canada — From American Indian word "Kannata" meaning "a number of settlers' huts". National Emblems — Maple Leaf, Beaver.

China — The word is said to have come from "Tsin", the ruler who built the Great Wall of China. National Emblem — Red Star.

England — Land of the Angles, who invaded and conquered South Britain in the 5th century. National Emblems — Lion, Rose, Bulldog.

France — (Old name Gaul — land of the Gauls). Present name from the Franks, who later conquered the country. National Emblems — Lily, Cock, Eagle.

Germany — "Germanus" (neighbours), a Roman word borrowed from the Gauls. Germans call their country "Deutschland". National Emblems — Eagle, Corn Flower.

India — The land through which the River Indus has its course. National Emblems — Elephant, Star, Lotus, Jasmine.

Ireland — (Gaelic name — Eire) — Land of the Irish tribe. National Emblems — Shamrock, Harp.

Italy — (= vitalia) — means "cattle or pasture land". National Emblems — Eagle, Lily, Laurel wreath.

Japan — The Japanese always use the word 'Nippon' and both mean "The Land of the Rising Sun". National Emblems — Chrysanthemum, Rising Sun.

New Zealand — (New Sea Land) — So named by a Dutch explorer after Zealand — a part of Holland. National Emblems — Kiwi, Fern.

Russia — Land of the tribe of Russ. National Emblems — Hammer and Sickle, Five-pointed Star.

Scotland — (Old name Caledonia). Present name from the Scots, a north of Ireland tribe, who invaded and gradually became masters of the whole country. National Emblems — Lion, Thistle.

South Africa — (see Africa). National Emblems — Springbok, Waggon.

Spain — English form of the word "Hispania" or "Espana". The name comes from "Shapan" (rabbit land), as the Phoenicians found the country over-run with these animals. National Emblems — Red Carnation, Pomegranate.

U.S.A. — (see America). National Emblems — Eagle, Buffalo, Golden Rod.

Turkey — Land of the Turks. National Emblems — Star and Crescent.

Wales — (Old name Cymru — land of the Cymri tribe). Present name is derived from Anglo-Saxon word meaning "land of the foreigner". National Emblems — Leek, Daffodil, Dragon.

VARIOUS COUNTRIES AND THEIR CAPITALS

Country	*Capital*	*Country*	*Capital*
Albania	Tirana	India	Delhi
Argentine	Buenos Aires	Israel	Tel Aviv
Australia	Canberra	Japan	Tokyo
Bangladesh	Dacca	New Zealand	Wellington
Brazil	Brasilia	Nigeria	Abuja
Bulgaria	Sofia	Norway	Oslo
Canada	Ottawa	Pakistan	Karachi
China	Beijin	Poland	Warsaw
Czechoslovakia	Prague	Portugal	Lisbon
Denmark	Copenhagen	Rumania	Bucharest
Egypt	Cairo	Russia	Moscow
Eire	Dublin	Scotland	Edinburgh
England	London	S. Africa	Cape Town
France	Paris	Spain	Madrid
Germany	Berlin	Sri Lanka	Colombo
Ghana	Accra	Sweden	Stockholm
Greece	Athens	Tasmania	Hobart
Holland	Amsterdam	Turkey	Ankara
Hungary	Budapest	United States	Washington
		Yugoslavia	Belgrade

CURRENCIES OF VARIOUS COUNTRIES

Argentine	peso, centavo	India	rupee, anna, pice
Australia	dollar, cent	Israel	shekel
Belgium	franc, centime	Italy	lira, centesimo
Britain	pound, pence	Japan	yen
Canada	dollar, cent	Mexico	peso, centavo
China	yuan, fen	Norway	krone, ore
Denmark	krone, ore	Poland	zloty, grosz
Egypt	pound, piastre	Portugal	escudo, centavo
France	franc, centime	Russia	rouble, kopeck
Germany	mark, pfennig	Switzerland	franc
Greece	drachma, lepton	Turkey	piastre, pound
Holland	guilder, cent	United States	dollar, cent

N.B. Some countries which are listed here are in the European Union, e.g., France and Germany, and are in the process of changing their currencies to the *Euro*.

DO YOU KNOW?

If there are any questions which you cannot answer, refer to an encyclopedia.

1. With which country or people each of the following is associated.

Ali	Foreign Legion	Midnight Sun	scimitar
Alphonse	Fritz	moccasins	shamrock
balmoral	Hans	Mounties	sombrero
beer	heather	mummies	tea
beret	ice-cream	onions	thistle
bolas	John Bull	oranges	tigers
boomerang	kangaroo	ostrich	tomahawk
butter	kilt	reindeer	tulips
cheese	lariat	rickshaw	turban
chopsticks	leek	Rising Sun	Uncle Sam
chrysanthemum	lotus flower	rose	vodka
clogs	macaroni	salmon	watches
daffodil	Marianne	sandals	whisky
fez	matches	Sandy	windmills

2. With which countries do you associate the following beasts of burden? Camel, dog, donkey, dromedary, elephant, horse, llama, mule, ox, reindeer, yak.

3. Who use (or used) the following kinds of boats? Canoe, coracle, dhow, galleon, gondola, junk, kayak, sampan.

4. What national names are often attached to the following? Example: **Scotch** broth. Baths, butter, cakes, carpets, cheese, drill, onions, sausage, stew, tea.

5. Who use (or used) these weapons? Boomerang, claymore, cutlass, harpoon, tomahawk, truncheon.

6. In what country would you be if your journey was called a safari, mush, hadj, trek?

7. With which country is each of the following names associated? Angus MacDonald, Tom Smith, Evan Jones, Patrick O'Neil, Chang Wu, Fritz Schmidt, Ivan Petrovitch, Juan Caballero, Pierre Sablon, Hans Brinker.

8. The town and country in which each is situated? Cleopatra's Needle, Colosseum, Eiffel Tower, Leaning Tower, Nelson's Monument, Pyramids, The Golden Gate, The Golden Horn, The Houses of Parliament, The Kremlin, The Pool, The Statue of Liberty, The Sphinx, The Taj Mahal, The Bridge of Sighs, The White House, The Vatican.

9. In which countries are the following mountains situated? Ben Nevis, Mt. Etna, Mt. Everest, Fujiyama, Mt. Blanc, Snowdon, Table Mountain, The Rockies, Vesuvius.

10. With which countries are the following famous people associated? Bonnie Prince Charlie, Buffalo Bill, Captain Cook, De Valera, General Franco, General Wolfe, George Washington, Gandhi, Haile Selassie, Hitler, Nelson, Peter the Great, Queen Victoria, Robert the Bruce, Roosevelt, The Kaiser, The Mikado, Wellington, William Tell, Stalin, Churchill, Chiang Kai-shek.

11. To what countries do the following names (seen on foreign stamps) apply? Argentina, Belgique, Danmark, Eire, Suomi, France, Deutschland, Nederland, Italia, Norge, Polska, Romania, Espana, Sverige, Suisse or Helvetia.

Part 3 — Tests

The answer to each question or help in answering it will be found in that Section which carries the same number as. the question, viz: **1.** Give the gender of dog — Section 1, Masculine. It is recommended that students attempt the whole test first and then check their answers from the relevant Section.

TEST 1

1. Give the gender of house, child, cow, sir.
2. Change all singulars into plurals: I heard the echo in the cave.
3. Write the following correctly: She had (gone, went) for a walk.
4. Write the following correctly: He is as heavy as (me, I).
5. Write the following correctly: She was the (older, oldest) of the two sisters.
6. Pick out the adverb in the following: He came early to get a good seat.
7. Put the correct preposition in the blank space: The boy lived .... a farm.
8. Join the following sentences together without using 'and', 'but' or 'so'. He works hard at his lessons. He wishes to succeed.
9. Pick out the subject in the following sentence: The soldier was wounded by the sniper.
10. Write the following correctly: Both you and I (have, has) heard the story.
11. Write the following correctly inserting apostrophe: The mens work was very hard.
12. Write the following correctly: i think that chelsea will win the cup.
13. Put into direct speech: John said that he was going home.
14. Complete the following: is cool as a ...., as soft as ....
15. Give the opposite of the following: success, visible, praise, transparent.
16. Give words similar in meaning to: comprehend, empty, acute, lofty.
17. Give words which sound the same as: allowed, grown, him, loan.
18. Form nouns from: accurate, cautious, clean, equal.
19. Give one name for the following: salmon, plaice, cod, flounder.
20. Put in order of size, smallest first: pound, stone, ounce, hundredweight, ton.
21. Complete the following: a .... of directors.
22. Complete the following: Day is to week as .... is to year.
23. Write in full: P.C., C.O.D., R.S.P.C.A., R.S.P.B.
24. Give the meaning of: 'under a cloud'.

TEST 2

1. Give the masculine of: hen, princess, spinster, niece.
2. Change all singulars into plurals: The lady spoke to the child.
3. Give the present tense of: I froze. I laughed. I ran. I spoke.
4. Write the following correctly: This argument is between you and (I, me).
5. Write the following correctly: Who is the (taller, tallest) John, George or Tom?
6. Write the following correctly: The boy ran (slow, slowly) up the hill.
7. Put the correct preposition in the blank space: The giant towered .... me
8. Join the following sentences together without using 'and', 'but' or 'so': The men were walking slowly. The men saw me.
9. Pick out the object in the following sentence: We have just bought a large house.
10. Write the following correctly: A man and some boys (was, were) cut off by the tide.
11. Write the following correctly inserting apostrophe: The ladies coats were left in the hall.
12. Write the following correctly: his name is george brown.
13. Put into direct speech: Mother told me that I would have to come with her.
14. Complete the following: as stiff as a ...., as light as a ....
15. Give the opposites of the following: arrive, nowhere, barren, ancient.
16. Give words similar in meaning to: moan, enemy, purchase, modern.
17. Give words which sound the same as: holy, rode, soot, paws.
18. Form adjectives from: child, destruction, ire, industry.
19. Give one name for the following: three, six, twelve, twenty.
20. Put in order of size, smallest first: sparrow, vulture, ostrich, hawk, blackbird.
21. Complete the following: a plague of ....
22. Complete the following: Island is to sea as .... is to land.
23. Write in full: B.Sc., C.I.D., P.O.
24. Give the meaning of: to sit on the fence.

TEST 3

1. Give the feminine of: hero, proprietor, host, son.
2. Change all singulars into plurals: The prisoner says that he is innocent.
3. Write the following correctly: He (saw, seen) his uncle yesterday.
4. Write the following correctly: This is the dog (who, which) bit me.
5. Write the following correctly: Peter weighed the (less, least) of us all.
6. Pick out the adverb in the following: Where did you get that toy?
7. Put the correct preposition in the blank space: The sailors rowed .... the bay.
8. Join the following sentences together without using 'and', 'but' or 'so': He heard music. He was passing the hall.
9. Pick out the subject in the following sentence: I met your father in the street.
10. Write the following correctly: The boy with his dog (was, were) waiting for me.
11. Write the following correctly inserting apostrophe: The horses mane was clipped short.
12. Write the following correctly: "we shall go out soon", john answered.
13. Put into indirect speech: "I want to see the game", said John.
14. Complete the following, as white as ....; as .... as the hills.
15. Give the opposites of the following: wise, audible, north, entrance
16. Give words similar in meaning to: marsh, annually, dampness, myth.
17. Give words which sound the same as: ball, herd, nose, mews.
18. Form verbs from: false, gold, just, obedient.
19. Give one name for the following: oil, gas, coal, paraffin.
20. Put in order of size, smallest first: shark, salmon, sole, pike, minnow.
21. Complete the following: a .... of herring.
22. Complete the following: hearing is to ear as sight is to ....
23. Write in full: B.S.T., do., N.A.T.O.
24. Give the meaning of: to rub the wrong way.

TEST 4

1. Give the gender of: sow, ram, owner, friend.
2. Change all singulars into plurals: The girl's hat was on the peg.
3. Write out the following using the correct part of the verb in brackets: Yesterday he .... at six o'clock (to rise).
4. Write the following correctly:, Let him and (I me) come with you.
5. Write the comparative and superlative of: famous, good, much.
6. Pick out the adverb in the following: The sun will be rising soon, he said.
7. Put the correct preposition in the blank space: We met them again .... the match.
8. Join the following sentences together without using 'and, 'but', or 'so': The lady lost the book. She was going to the library.
9. Pick out the object in the following sentence: The golfer won a magnificent cup.
10. Write the following correctly: The boy and his dog (was, were) going for a walk.
11. Write the following correctly, inserting apostrophe: It took many days work to build the garage.
12. Write the following correctly: the prime minister entered the house of commons.
13. Put into indirect speech: "When did you arrive home?" my father asked.
14. Complete the following: as strong as a ....; as .... as a puppy.
15. Give the opposites of the following: behave, rough, pedestrian, known.
16. Give words similar in meaning to: conversation, strong, coax, prohibit.
17. Give words which sound the same as: fool, sight, peer, steal.
18. Form nouns from: marry, pacify, please, laugh.
19. Pick the odd one out of the following: captain, sergeant, private, admiral, general.
20. Put in order of size, smallest first: melon, orange, raisin, plum, grape.
21. Complete the following: a .... of oxen.
22. Complete the following: Flock is to sheep as .... is to cattle.
23. Write in full: Prof., Y.M.C.A., C.
24. Give the meaning of: 'as the crow flies'.

TEST 5

1. Give the masculine of: bitch, tigress, bride, heiress.
2. Change all singulars into plurals: His tooth hurt him badly.
3. Change the verbs into the present tense: I made sure he saw me.
4. Write the following correctly: (Her, She) and I get on well together.
5. Correct the following: This wall is more long than the opposite one.
6. Correct the following: He wrote very bad for a boy of his age.
7. Put the correct preposition in the blank space: The prisoner was held .... the wall and searched.
8. Join the following sentences together without using 'and', 'but' or 'so': The boy was a rascal. I couldn't help liking him.
9. Pick out the subject in the following sentence: After the dance they walked home.
10. Write the following correctly: Most of the group (was, were) present.
11. Write the following correctly, inserting apostrophe: Mrs. Jones bag was stolen.
12. Write the following correctly: her mother took jean to see the queen.
13. Put into direct speech: My mother asked if I was afraid of the dentist.
14. Complete the following: as mad as a ....; as .... as a fox.
15. Give the opposites of the following: legible, guilty, possible, often.
16. Give words similar in meaning to: mute, profit, calamity, enormous.
17. Give words which sound the same as: gilt, higher, meat, tears.
18. Form adjectives from: sense, service, spirit, wit.
19. Pick out the one word from *(b)* which is the same as those in *(a)*:
    (a) finch, sparrow, eagle. *(b)* fly, giraffe, hawk, gnu.
20. Put in order of size, smallest first: book, chapter, sentence, word, page.
21. Complete the following: a .... of cards.
22. Complete the following: .... is to fish as air is to animal.
23. Write in full: A.A., R.A.C., e.g.
24. Give the meaning of: 'the lion's share'.

TEST 6

1. Give the feminine of: duke, uncle, sir, waiter.
2. Change all plurals into singulars: The boys robbed birds' nests.
3. Write the following correctly: He was (awoke, awakened) by the noise.
4. Write the following correctly: The cat got up and stretched (its, it's) legs.
5. Write the following correctly: Peter is not the (thinner, thinnest) boy in the class.
6. Write the following correctly: Would you walk as (quick, quickly) as you can?
7. Put the correct preposition in the blank space: We ran happily .... the river bank.
8. Join the following sentences together without using 'and', 'but' or 'so': Please let me know. You wish to go.
9. Pick out the object in the following sentence. Sobbing quietly, she told her story.
10. Write the following correctly: (Does, Do) James and George know the truth?
11. Write the following correctly, inserting apostrophe: He looked very proud in his soldiers uniform.
12. Write the following correctly: father and david were going to london.
13. Put into direct speech: Peter asked William if he was going out.
14. Complete the following: as .... as a lark; as clear as ....
15. Give the opposites of the following: modest, enemy, noble, bitter.
16. Give words similar in meaning to: sign, surround, fatigue, reveal.
17. Give words which sound the same as: leak, council, peel, sole.
18. Form verbs from: variety, advertisement, behaviour, courage.
19. Pick out the one word from *(b)* which means the same as those in *(a)* :
    (a) amaze, shock, surprise *(b)* deceive, gaze, astonish, grasp.
20. Put in order of size, smallest first: lettuce, beetroot, turnip, pea, potato.
21. Complete the following: a .... of corn.
22. Complete the following: Tear is to sorrow as smile is to ....
23. Write in full: Lieut., E.E.C., P.T.O.
24. Give the meaning of: 'to show a clean pair of heels'.

TEST 7

1. Give the gender of: adult, duck, heifer, chair.
2. Change all singulars into plurals: The angler caught a salmon.
3. Write the following correctly: I was sure that he had (forgotten, forgot).
4. Write the following correctly: The bully chased Tom and (me, I).
5. Write the comparative and superlative of: hot, beautiful.
6. Correct the following: This job can be done very easy.
7. Put the correct preposition in the blank space: He arrived early .... the school.
8. Join the following sentences together without using 'and', 'but' or 'so': I have asked him twice. He has not replied.
9. Pick out the object in the following sentence: The soldier dropped his rifle with a clatter.
10. Write the following correctly:, One of the planes (was, were) missing.
11. Write the following correctly: He didnt know what to do.
12. Write the following correctly: i think that reach for the sky is a marvellous book.
13. Put into indirect speech: "Mary, what are you looking for?", asked Joan.
14. Complete the following: as sweet as ....; as .... as a daisy.
15. Give the opposites of the following: senior, obedient, bright, regular.
16. Give words similar in meaning to: nimble, peculiar, wander, smooth.
17. Give words which sound the same as: plaice, threw, fair, ate.
18. Form nouns from: discover, freeze, imitate, judge.
19. Give one name for the following: hammer, saw, chisel, drill.
20. Put in order of size, smallest first: half, one, third, fifth, tenth.
21. Complete the following: a .... of furniture.
22. Complete the following: Foot is to man as .... is to horse.
23. Write in full: H.R.H., A.D., Lab.
24. Give the meaning of: 'a flash in the pan'.

TEST 8

1. Change all feminines into masculines: The manageress asked the girl to count her change again.
2. Change all plurals into singulars: They wrote our names.
3. Change the following verbs into the present tense: I had run, I was throwing, I knelt, I left
4. Write the following correctly: If you tried, you and (he, him) could be friends.
5. Write the comparative and superlative of: little, cautious, tall.
6. Pick out the adverb in the following sentence: We did not attend the game.
7. Put the correct preposition in the blank space: He looked .... the garden before he entered the house.
8. Join the following sentences together without using 'and', 'but' or 'so': Let us go home. We have finished.
9. Pick out the subject in the following sentence: We sat down beside an old man.
10. Write the following correctly: All of us but Tom (is, are) going to the game.
11. Write the following correctly: My daughters doll lay in its cot.
12. Write the following correctly: i have never seen peter pan performed.
13. Put into indirect speech: "I wonder where that path goes?", said Alex.
14. Complete the following: as flat as a ....; as .... as a deer.
15. Give the opposites of the following: sense, heavy, stormy, pleasant.
16. Give the words similar in meaning to: quantity, position, strict, noted.
17. Give words which sound the same as: cereal, maid, their, waste.
18. Form adjectives from: lose, mountain, pity, reason.
19. Give one name for the following: Moscow, Beijing, Accra, Delhi.
20. Put in order of size, smallest first: socks, jacket, coat, shirt, tie.
21. Complete the following: a .... of islands.
22. Complete the following: Artist is to .... as author is to book.
23. Write in full: Gen., I.M.F., R.C.
24. Give the meaning of: 'to play with fire'.

TEST 9

1. Give the masculine of: widow, tailoress, grandmother.
2. Change all singulars into plurals: The thief tried to enter my house.
3. Write the following correctly: We had (wrote, written) a letter.
4. Write the following correctly: I wonder if he will let Tom and (I, me) go with him.
5. Correct the following: Of the two, I dislike James most.
6. Pick out the adverb in the following: We have been here at a previous time.
7. Put the correct preposition in the blank space: The farmer walked .... the horse and cart.
8. Join the following sentences without using 'and', 'but' or 'so': He failed the test. He was careless.
9. Pick out the subject in the following sentence: Of the two resorts, I prefer the smaller.
10. Write the following correctly: William and Peter (go, goes) to the pictures every week.
11. Write the following correctly: You cant make me do this.
12. Write the following correctly: he asked me, "do you think i was right?".
13. Put into direct speech:, My father asked me whether my team had won.
14. Complete the following: as proud as a ....; as .... as a rock.
15. Give the opposites of the following: dark, beautiful, ascent, temporary.
16. Give words similar in meaning to: dusk, exterior, gap, saluted.
17. Give words which sound the same as: week, rye, real, hew.
18. Form verbs from: sad, speech, sympathy, width.
19. Pick the odd one out of the following: butter, cheese, margarine, yogurt.
20. Put in order of size, smallest first: yacht, dinghy, canoe, liner, speedboat.
21. Complete the following: a .... of cubs.
22. Complete the following: One is to single as two is to ....
23. Write in full: Col., w.w.w., A.A.
24. Give the meaning of: 'to strike while the iron is hot'.

TEST 10

1. Give the feminine of: friar, him, priest, colt.
2. Change all plurals into singulars: We waited for them outside the shops.
3. Write the following correctly: The horse has (broken, broke) its leg in the fall.
4. Write the following correctly: George and (he, him) are sworn enemies.
5. Write the following correctly: William is the (slower, slowest) runner of us all.
6. Correct the following: James didn't speak very clear.
7. Put the correct preposition in the blank space: He fell on to the rocks .... the cliffs.
8. Join the following sentences without using 'and', 'but' or 'so': You should not break the rules. You do not want to be punished.
9. Pick out the object in the following sentence: Before the operation he made his will.
10. Write the following correctly: Mary and Jean (give, gives) their mother a lot of trouble.
11. Write the following correctly: The babies cots were lined up in a row.
12. Write the following correctly: the birthplace of robert burns is near ayr.
13. Put into direct speech: My friend Bob asked me to come to the pictures with him.
14. Complete the following: as .... as iron; as cold as ....
15. Give the opposites of the following: purchased, lazy, abundance, intelligent.
16. Give words similar in meaning to: regret, slender, halt, heroic.
17. Give words which sound the same as: ceiling, knot, muscle, steak.
18. Form nouns from: absent, broad, choose, deep.
19. Pick the odd one out of the following: sausage, bacon, steak, liver.
20. Write down the two words in the brackets which are associated with the first word: House: (carpet, box, hall, marble, top).
21. Complete the following: a .... of grass.
22. Complete the following: Nose is to smell as .... is to taste.
23. Write in full: w.w.w., H.M.S., I.T.A.
24. Give the meaning of: 'a storm in a teacup'.

TEST 11

1. Give the gender of: drake, mare, knife, pupil.
2. Change all singulars into plurals: The sheep tried to escape from its pen.
3. Write out the following using the correct part of the verb in brackets: The boy .... under the hedge and waited. (to lie).
4. Write the following correctly: This is the boy (which, who) fell in the river.
5. Write the following correctly: Peter is the (worse, worst) behaved boy I know.
6. Write the following correctly: He talked (louder, more loudly) than anyone.
7. Put the correct preposition in the blank space: The driveway ran .... the house.
8. Join the following sentences without using, 'and', 'but' or 'so': The hours went by. We grew more and more anxious.
9. Pick out the subject in the following sentence: It was a neat little house.
10. Write the following correctly: All but one of the boys (run, runs) well.
11. Write the following correctly: I hope youre sure of your facts.
12. Write the following correctly: guy fawkes' day is in november.
13. Put into indirect speech: "Is this the right road for London?" the stranger asked me.
14. Complete the following: as .... as a mouse; as tender as a ....
15. Give the opposites of the following: rough, question, empty, polite.
16. Give words similar in meaning to: blamed, stick, blank, circular.
17. Give words which sound the same as: wait, read, pair, blew.
18. Form adjectives from: divide, exhaust, force, grieve.
19. Pick out the word from *(b)* which means the same as those in *(a)* :
    (a) thrust, pushed, shoved *(b)* jerked, glanced, pressed, touched.
20. Write the two words in the brackets which are associated with the first word: Book: (hands, blade, title, cover, tool).
21. Complete the following: a .... of stars.
22. Complete the following: Rich is to poor as ancient is to ....
23. Write in full: H.M., M.D., a.m.
24. Give the meaning of: 'to play the game'.

TEST 12

1. Change all masculines into feminines: After a long chase he caught his runaway stallion.
2. Change all plurals into singulars: The mice ate the pieces of cheese in the traps.
3. Write out the following using the correct part of the verb in brackets: He was .... to realise that he was lost (to begin).
4. Write the following correctly: He is as fond of food as (I, me).
5. Write the comparative and superlative of: far, generous, handsome.
6. Pick out the adverbs in the following: There lay the men sleeping peacefully.
7. Put the correct preposition in the blank space: The hedge lay .... the two gardens.
8. Join the following sentences without using 'and', 'but' or 'so': We were on our way home. It began to rain heavily.
9. Pick out the subject in the following sentence: Standing motionless, we returned their gaze with interest.
10. Write the following correctly: One of the books (was, were) destroyed.
11. Write the following correctly: The boys book lay on the teachers desk.
12. Write the following correctly: you'll pay for that, robert said.
13. Put into indirect speech: "I have been playing in the park," Mary told me.
14. Complete the following: as sharp as a ....; as .... as glass.
15. Give the opposites of the following: morning, rise, east, hero.
16. Give words similar in meaning to: menace, least, mischief, odour.
17. Give words which sound the same as: board, night, missed, sore.
18. Form verbs from: glory, injury, knowledge, success.
19. Pick out the word from *(b)* which belongs to the same group as those from *(a)* : *(a)* lawyer, clerk, judge, *(b)* client, prisoner, solicitor, policeman.
20. Write down the two words in the brackets which are associated with the first word: Grocer: (fish, fruit, cheese, meat, soup).
21. Complete the following: a .... of bells.
22. Complete the following: Wrist is to arm as ankle is to ....
23. Write in full: E.U., M.P., A.A.A.
24. Give the meaning of: 'to throw in the cards'.

TEST 13

1. Give the masculine of: female, goddess, vixen, she.
2. Change all singulars into plurals: The fly was trapped in the spider's web.
3. Write out the following correctly: The visitor (rang, rung) our bell.
4. Write the following correctly: The angry supporters gathered round (he, him) and (I, me).
5. Write the positive and comparative of: thinnest, best, most comfortable.
6. Write the following correctly: He walked (slower, more slowly) than I did.
7. Put the correct preposition in the blank space: The enchanted island lay .... the horizon.
8. Join the following sentences without using 'and', 'but' or 'so': He said that he was very sorry. I let him off with a warning.
9. Pick out the object in the following sentence: Read the passage carefully before beginning.
10. Write the following correctly: Only one of the boys (like, likes) singing.
11. Write the following correctly: "Theres no time to waste," he said.
12. Write the following correctly: the famous explorer, david livingstone, was born in blantyre.
13. Put into direct speech: He told us that we would have to work harder.
14. Complete the following: as .... as sin; as pale as ....
15. Give the opposites of the following: fancy, big, profit, superior.
16. Give words similar in meaning to: tested, mariner, painful, forbid.
17. Give words which sound the same as: sweet, won, sail, profit.
18. Form nouns from: able, apply, breathe, content.
19. Give one name for the following: snake, lizard, crocodile, alligator.
20. Write down the two words in the brackets which are associated with the first word: School: (car, glass, desk, year, term).
21. Complete the following: a .... of horses.
22. Complete the following: .... is to herring as school is to whales.
23. Write in full: Maj;. LL.B., No.
24. Give the meaning of: 'good for nothing'.

TEST 14

1. Give the gender of: relative, singer, mirror, farmer.
2. Change all plurals into singulars: The cities were destroyed by the armies.
3. Write out the following using the correct part of the verb in brackets: The enemy .... creeping up on us (to come).
4. Write the following correctly: The man watched (they, them) closely.
5. Write the positive and superlative of: more certain, worse, later.
6. Pick out the adverbs in the following: Now is the time to strike quickly.
7. Put the correct preposition in the blank space: The attack took me .... surprise.
8. Join the following sentences without using 'and', 'but' or 'so': You have worked very hard. You deserve a rest.
9. Pick out the subject in the following sentence: The leaf of this tree is bright yellow.
10. Write the following correctly: Both the boy and the girl (is, are) to be presented with a medal.
11. Write the following correctly: My fathers car was stolen.
12. Write the following correctly: the continent of australia was discovered by captain cook.
13. Put into direct speech: My friend asked me where I was going for my holidays.
14. Complete the following: as .... as a rake; as sour as ....
15. Give the opposites of the following: rich, mighty, advance, success.
16. Give words similar in meaning to: protect, request, unite, wrath.
17. Give words which sound the same as: scene, nun, gate, boy.
18. Form adjectives from: create, darkness, education, fortune.
19. Give one name for the following: coal, shirt, scarf, hat.
20. Write down the two words in the brackets which are associated with the first word: Television: (book, screen, artist, aerial, light).
21. Complete the following: a .... of rags.
22. Complete the following: One is to dozen as dozen is to ....
23. Write in full: Rev., M.A., O.H.M.S.
24. Give the meaning of: 'carried away'.

TEST 15

1. Give the feminine of: bachelor, nephew, gander, stag.
2. Change all singulars into plurals: The glass was on the shelf.
3. Write the following correctly: We had (driven, drove) for miles out of our way.
4. Write the following correctly: At the end of the meeting the chairman thanked (we, us).
5. Correct the following: A more fast car I have never seen,
6. Write the following correctly: He understood the problem (most clearly, clearest) of all.
7. Put the correct preposition in the blank space: The girls walked happily .... the hall.
8. Join the following sentences without using 'and', 'but' or 'so': He did not take any cake. There was not enough for everyone.
9. Pick out the object in the following sentence: He showed me into a small room.
10. Write the following correctly: The band (was, were) playing a catchy tune.
11. Write the following correctly: The boys heads were bowed in silence.
12. Write the following correctly: when in london we visited st paul's cathedral.
13. Put into indirect speech: "Have you been to Canada before?" Peter asked me.
14. Complete the following: As keen as ....; as .... as a sheet.
15. Give the opposites of the following: export, feeble, conceal, arrive.
16. Give words similar in meaning to: lean, margin, ancient, cautious.
17. Give words which sound the same as: beer, course, know, right.
18. Form verbs from: hatred, height, large, life.
19. Pick the odd one out of the following: wool, silk, nylon, cotton, linen.
20. Write down the two words in the brackets which are associated with the first word: Theatre: (candles, stage, lighting, glass, mirror).
21. Complete the following: a .... of pictures.
22. Complete the following: .... is to cold as seldom is to often.
23. Write in full: Q.C., B.C., v.
24. Give the meaning of: 'to hit the nail on the head'.

TEST 16

1. Change all feminines into masculines: She asked the stewardess if she could change her seat.
2. Change all plurals into singulars: The cows gave birth to calves.
3. Write out the following using the correct part of the verb in brackets: I made sure that he .... wisely (to choose).
4. Write the following correctly: I don't think you and (he, him) can do it.
5. Correct the following: I have never met a badder boy than Tom.
6. Pick out the adverbs in the following: 'I will certainly come immediately", he said briskly.
7. Put the correct preposition in the blank space: The fire broke out .... the night.
8. Join the following sentences without using 'and', 'but' or 'so': I rang the bell. A little girl came to the door.
9. Pick out the subject in the following sentence: I left the office before five o'clock.
10. Write the following correctly: The leader and his men (was, were) going to leave.
11. Write the following correctly: "Surely thats not all", he said.
12. Write the following correctly: after his defeat at waterloo, napoleon was exiled to st helena.
13. Put into indirect speech: "We can't go any further on this path", our guide said.
14. Complete the following: as hungry as a ....; as .... as an owl.
15. Give the opposites of the following: present, bitter, danger, lost.
16. Give the words similar in meaning to: option, custom, cunning, elude.
17. Give words which sound the same as: hole, maize, tail, tolled.
18. Form nouns from: mourn, occupy, see, soft.
19. Pick the odd one out of the following: eagle, hawk, owl, robin, falcon.
20. Write down the words in brackets which are associated with the first word: Artist: (easel, spoon, light, palette, cloak).
21. Complete the following: a .... of insects.
22. Complete the following: Wheel is to spoke as flower is to ....
23. Write in full: Capt., R.N., G.M.T.
24. Give the meaning of: 'to mind your p's and q's'.

TEST 17

1. Give the gender of: sheep, guest, table, companion.
2. Change all singulars into plurals: The ox hauled the heavy load.
3. Write the following correctly: They (swum, swam) out to the rocks.
4. Write the following correctly: The prize will go to you or (he, him).
5. Write the comparative and superlative of: great, thin, many.
6. Pick out the adverbs in the following: For an old man, he walked quite quickly.
7. Put the correct preposition in the blank space: I received my order .... the grocer's shop.
8. Join the following sentences without using 'and', 'but' or 'so': The boy was crossing the river. He fell into the water.
9. Pick out the object in the following sentence: Before leaving, he gave me a present.
10. Write the following correctly: Bob, like Jack, (is, are) not always polite.
11. Write the following correctly: The shoppers cars were all parked at meters.
12. Write the following correctly: "that's a fine gun you've got", william told john.
13. Put into direct speech: The gamekeeper warned us that we were trespassing.
14. Complete the following: as meek as a ....; as ....as a mouse.
15. Give the opposites of the following: defend, strange, throw, new.
16. Give words similar in meaning to: fall, hearth, insolent, maximum.
17. Give words which sound the same as: pores, key, lair, cord.
18. Form adjectives from: shade, skill, value, wood.
19. Give one name for the following: baker, dentist, joiner, clerk.
20. Write down the two words in the brackets which are associated with the first word: Football: (jacket, referee, switch, team, unit).
21. Complete the following: a .... of mice.
22. Complete the following: Graceful is to .... as polite is to rude.
23. Write in full: J.P., I.O.U., Ltd.
24. Give the meaning of: 'back to the wall'.

TEST 18

1. Change all masculines into feminines: The savage tiger attacked the helpless buck.
2. Change all plurals into singulars: The women paid for their messages.
3. Write out the following using the correct part of the verb in brackets: I do not know where he .... the stolen property. (to hide).
4. Write the following correctly: The final will be played between (they, them) and (we, us).
5. Write the comparative and superlative of: ignorant, far, bad.
6. Write the following correctly: The rearguard fought (more bravely, braver) than anyone.
7. Put the correct preposition in the blank space: We listened to him .... silence.
8. Join the following sentences without using 'and', 'but' or 'so': After his walk he was so tired. He fell asleep in the chair.
9. Pick out the subject in the following sentence: Looking back, he realised his mistake.
10. Write the following correctly: All of the girls (play, plays) netball very well.
11. Write the following correctly: 'I dont think its in the right place". I said.
12. Write the following correctly: the eiffel tower in paris is a wonderful building.
13. Put into direct speech: The crowd demanded their money back.
14. Complete the following: as .... as Punch; as slow as a ....
15. Give the opposites of the following: die, stale, deny, famous.
16. Give words similar in meaning to: quaint, shrine, small, stubborn.
17. Give words which sound the same as: altar, bough, hall, mail.
18. Form verbs from: weak, assistance, camp, deed.
19. Give one name for the following: basket ball, netball, tennis, golf.
20. Write down the two words in the brackets which are associated with the word Medicine. (tanker, bottle, drug, captain)
21. Complete the following: a .... of whales.
22. Complete the following: Whisper is to shout as walk is to ....
23. Write in full: H.P., kph, R.I.P.
24. Give the meaning of: 'to send to Coventry'.

TEST 19

1. Give the feminine of: emperor, brave, masseur, executor
2. Change all singulars into plurals: The man ate a large potato.
3. Change all verbs in the following sentence into the present tense: He was following me wherever I went.
4. Write the following correctly: Did she tell you about (they, them)
5. Correct the following: Who is the smallest, John or Betty?
6. Pick out the adverbs in the following: We met him before the accident but we have not seen him since.
7. Put the correct preposition in the blank space:, We do not live .... the sea.
8. Join the following sentences without using 'and', 'but' or 'so'. He was running to catch a train. I did not stop him.
9. Pick out the object in the following sentence: After lunch, we played football.
10. Write the following correctly: The officer, like his men, (was, were) wearing full uniform.
11. Write the following correctly: The childrens toys lay in a tangled heap.
12. Write the following correctly: we have never visited norway or sweden.
13. Put into indirect speech: "help me to climb over the wall", John asked me.
14. Complete the following: as .... as a horse; as proud as a ....
15. Give the opposites of the following: narrow, contract, frown, normal.
16. Give words similar in meaning to: remedy, suspend, terror, wretched.
17. Give words which sound the same as: dear, hear, core, loot.
18. Form nouns from: deceive, depart, enter, free.
19. Pick the odd one out of the following: lead, iron, aluminium, silver, gold.
20. Write down the two words in the brackets which are associated with the first word: Cutlery: (jar, spoon, kettle, cup, fork).
21. Complete the following: a .... of birds.
22. Complete the following: Wrist is to cuff as .... is to collar.
23. Write in full: R.S.P.C.A., O.K., S.A.
24. Give the meaning of: 'a fly in the ointment'.

TEST 20

1. Give the gender of: orphan, bullock, witch, swan.
2. Change all singulars into plurals: The deer was grazing on the hillside.
3. Write the following correctly: I did not know that he had (grew, grown) a beard.
4. Write the following correctly: We fell silent when (he, him) and his friend appeared.
5. State whether the following are positive, comparative, or superlative: surest, larger, certain.
6. Pick out the adverbs in the following: I saw him once before he won the race easily.
7. Put the correct preposition in the blank space: The fugitive swam .... the nearest ship.
8. Join the following sentences without using 'and', 'but' or 'so': I entered the room. I looked out of the window.
9. Pick out the subject in the following sentence: George decided to go to bed.
10. Write the following correctly: Not one of us (is, are) using the old machine.
11. Write the following correctly: The boys jacket was torn.
12. Write the following correctly: jim said, "have you ever read treasure island?" "no", i replied.
13. Put into direct speech: The accused said that he was innocent.
14. Complete the following: as safe as the ....; as .... as grass.
15. Give the opposites of the following: multiply, youth, correct, necessary.
16. Give words similar in meaning to: protect, myth, rapid, surrender.
17. Give words which sound the same as: vain, crews, mare, rose.
18. Form adjectives from: hope, inform, move, poison.
19. Pick the odd one out of the following: trout, lobster, herring, sole, halibut.
20. Write down the two words in the brackets which are associated with the first word: Crockery: (knife, bowl, saucer, bottle, rung.)
21. Complete the following: a .... of runners.
22. Complete the following: .... is to forest as sheep is to flock.
23. Write in full: M.A., U.K., V.I.P.
24. Give the meaning of: 'to take a rise out of'.

INDEX

	Section S / Page P		Section S / Page P
Abbreviations	S 23	Formation of Adjectives	S 5
Adjectives	S 5	Formation of Verbs	S 3
Adverbs	S 6	Formation of Adverbs	S 6
Agreement between subject and verb	S 10	Gender	S 1
Analogies	S 22	Group names	S 21
Antonyms	S 15	Homes	P 60
Anybody	S 10	Homonyms	S 17
Apostrophe	S 11	I, me	S 4
Association	S 20	Indirect Speech	S 13
Auxiliary verbs	S 3	Its, It's	S 4
Capital Letters	S 12	Language	P 70
Capitals of Countries	P 72	Masculine Nouns	S 1
Classification	S 19	Me, I	S 4
Collective Nouns	S 1	Metaphors	S 14
Colloquial Expressions	S 24	Neither, either	S 10
Colloquialisms	S 24	Neither, nor	S 10
Common Nouns	S 1	Neither of	S 10
Comparison of Adjectives	S 5	Neuter Nouns	S 1
Comparison of Adverbs	S 6	Nobody	S 10
Comparative degree of adjectives	S 5	None	S 10
Comparative degree of adverbs	S 6	Not one of	S 10
Concord	S 10	Nouns (collective)	S 1
Conjunctions	S 8	Nouns (common)	S 1
Countries	P 69	Nouns (feminine)	S 1
Currencies	P 72	Nouns (masculine)	S 1
Degree of comparison of adjectives	S 5	Nouns (neuter)	S 1
Degrees of comparison of adverbs	S 6	Nouns (proper)	S 1
Derivations	P 56	Object	S 2
Direct Speech	S 13	Occupation	P 61
Each	S 10	Of, off	S 12
Each of	S 10	One of	S 10
Either, neither	S 10	Opposites	S 15
Either, or	S 10	Opposites by changing prefix	S 15
Every	S 10	Opposites by changing suffix	S 15
Everybody	S 10	Origins of words	P 56
Every one of	S 10	Parents and young	P 59
Families	P 59	Parts of Speech	S 1/8
Feminine Nouns	S 1	Parts of the Verb	S 2
Figures of Speech	S 14	Past Participle	S 3
Formation of Nouns	S 1	Past Tense	S 3

	Section S / Page P			Section S / Page P
Peoples of the World	P 70	Similar words (in meaning)	S 16
Personal Pronouns	S 4	Similar words (in sound)	S 17
Place name, origin of	P 70	Similies	S 14
Plural nouns	S 2	Singular and plural	S 2
Popular Phrases	S 24	Spelling lists	P 64
Positive degree of adjectives	S 5	Subject	S 9
Positive degree of adverbs	S 6	Suffixes	P 58
Possessive Case	S 4	Superlative degree of adjectives	S 5
Prefixes	P 57	Superlative degree of adverbs	S 6
Prepositions	S 7	Synonyms	S 16
Present participles	S 3	Tenses	S 3
Present tense	S 3	Their, there	S 17
Pronouns (personal)	S 4	To, too, two	S 17
Pronouns (relative)	S 4	Verbs	S 3
Pronouns as object	S 4	Verbs (auxiliary)	S 3
Pronouns as subject	S 4	Who, whom	S 4
Pronouns (common errors)	S 4	Whose, who's	S 4
Proper nouns	S 1	Word building	S 18
Proverbs	P 53	Words which mean the opposite	S 15
Races of Mankind	P 68	Words which mean the same	S 16
Relative pronouns	S 4	Words which sound the same	S 17
Roots of words	P 56		

Printed by Martins the Printers, Ltd.,
Berwick upon Tweed, Scotland.